The Journey of Life

100 Lessons from Around the World

by Sharon K. Sobotta

This first edition of
The Journey of Life: 100 Lessons from Around the World by **Sharon K. Sobotta**
is published by: **Channel Trade Editions**
and distributed by: **SCB Distributors**
15608 South New Century Drive
Gardena, California 90248
P: 310-532-9400
Concept by: **Sharon K. Sobotta, Intercultural Encounters**
www.interculturalencounters.com

Cover Designed by: **Saima Haque**
Book Designed by: **Deepak Srivastava, Nirvana Media Group, Inc.**
Copy Edits by: **Nirmala Nataraj**

ISBN:0-9793801-4-6
  978-0-9793801-4-3

Table of Contents

*E*ngaging in Life   14
      Living passionately and nourishing your soul

*M*obilizing, Mentoring & Motivating   46
      Inspiring others and setting an example

*P*racticing What You Preach   66
      Staying in touch with your roots and living your ideologies

*O*vercoming Obstacles & Stereotypes   86
      Being the best that you can be

*W*aiting   104
      Understanding the virtues of patience and compromise

*E*mpathizing with the World   116
      Relating to people from all walks of life

*R*eciprocating   140
      Mastering the art of giving, taking and appreciating

*U*niversal Truths to Live By   154

Dedicated to:

Mrs. Patricia Thorsbakken and all the teachers
who change lives every day,

Tricia Mae, for being the most incredible sister in
the whole world,

Sanjib, for encouraging me to write this book,

All of the people who shared their stories
and inspired me,

And every one who dares to think with their heart
and pursue their dreams.

Preface

I grew up in a working-class family in a town of 1,500 in West Central Wisconsin. My dad, a janitor by profession, struggled with bipolar manic depression for as long as I can remember, while my mom did her best to take care of the family on the salary of an elementary-school teacher. I wasn't sure what my purpose was or where I fit into the world. I got along with everyone at school, but didn't have a definite home in any clique of friends. I hung around with the "group-home kids" and with the "good kids," but never at the same time. I was the one who teachers assigned to help the new students fit in. I knew there was a larger world out there, but wasn't sure how to access it.

In high school, I had one teacher, Mrs. Thorsbakken, who inspired me to find my way. She was a petite woman with black, bobbed hair, and ironically taught home economics, the subject I was most apathetic about. Mrs. Thorsbakken never gave up on me—she pushed me to do my best, to care, to get involved and to believe in myself. When I was seventeen, she encouraged me to apply for a Kikkoman Soy Sauce scholarship to spend a summer in Japan. Knowing nothing about Japan, I accepted the challenge as a chance to experience life outside of Wisconsin. A few months later, I was transplanted to the heart of Tokyo.

When I arrived at Narita Airport on my first trip to Japan, as a chubby-cheeked, naïve, insecure seventeen-year-old girl, with embarrassingly natural blonde permed hair and an unfashionably awkward outfit, I was like a fish out of water. I was wearing a pink jumper dress with blue and white square patches and a white t-shirt underneath with matching white socks and baby-doll black shoes.

A small woman with glasses and broccoli-shaped hair named Keiko and her daughter Minako had come to meet me. Keiko and Minako had been designated my host mother and host sister for the summer. The two of them led me to my new home via the train.

Trudging up never-ending flights of stairs with my large carry-on bag, a backpack and a suitcase, I struggled to keep up with Keiko and Minako. On the patches of ground that separated the staircases from each other and the stairs from the train, I managed to tip my suitcase over at least once every three strides. I was too exhausted to be excited, but intrigued by the uncertainty of the symbols, the pace and everything around me. Unlike me, everyone seemed to know exactly where they were going. I kept an ear-to-ear smile painted on my face and randomly greeted individuals, "konichiwa," when their eyes met mine. Once inside the train, Keiko began pointing at her nose and speaking to me in Japanese. I stared blankly at her. Her daughter Minako intervened with some broken English as she tried to explain the train, the people, her school and her city. By now, the muscles in my face began to tense up, making it harder for me to hold onto my smile. As I strained my ears to listen and my mind to focus, I knew it would be a long summer. What I did not know on the seemingly endless train ride was that the experiences I would encounter over the next six weeks would change my life. Not only would I be inspired to learn Japanese, I would develop an incurable desire to travel the world. I would discover the priceless value of inquisitiveness that would later inspire me to become a journalist. Most importantly, I would develop an irreversible sense of resiliency and flexibility to help me get through all of life's most difficult moments.

The Birth of
The Journey of Life: 100 Lessons from Around the World

I once heard the process of writing a book compared to the process of giving birth. I have not yet had the privilege of bringing a child into the world, so I have no way of confirming this—but I imagine it to be an understatement.

It all started in December 2005. I had moved three times that year: first, to escape a less than ideal roommate situation in Walnut Creek; next, to a larger apartment in East Oakland, along with two new roommates; and finally, to a one-bedroom apartment in downtown Oakland. My Suzuki Esteem, which I had proudly claimed as the cheapest car on the market (even, ironically, bragging about how lucky I was to own a car that no one would ever be interested in breaking into), had been broken into five times already. That year, my neighbors had been robbed at gunpoint, I had watched a person get run over and gunshots had become an all too familiar background noise. Moreover, there was no coffeeshop in walking distance for me to engage in my passions of people-watching and writing over hot tea.

I was approaching the last years of my twenties, and it was clear that the blueprint I'd based my entire life on was not going to materialize into anything more than a "plan." Upon moving to my newest, safest apartment, my prized possession—my laptop computer—was stolen from my apartment. The man I had handed my heart to moved to LA and suggested we "undefine" our relationship. My dream of being a career woman, along with having a supportive husband and a child or two by the age of 30, would not be realized within my projected time frame. I felt as if I was being tested by the universe.

Then, it occurred to me. While I didn't have all the concrete markers of success I had idealized, I did lead a life that many only dreamed about. I had traveled the world on a shoestring budget and lived among, studied alongside and interviewed people from every walk of life imaginable. I loved that my status as a journalist had given me a free pass to interview, pry, ask endless questions and collect the life stories of others. It served as an excuse to be a temporary resident of whatever destination I was in, as a non-tourist. (While I had always loved the serendipity and satisfaction of setting up temporary roots in a new location, I had never been a fan of visiting museums, taking tours or even the actual process of traveling—thanks in part to my travel sickness and fear of flying.)

I began my global journey when I was just seventeen, after being awarded a scholarship from Kikkoman Soy Sauce to leave Wisconsin and go to Japan for a summer. That trip turned into a game of "life dominoes." It inspired me to learn Japanese and return to Japan as a college student. My trip back to Japan in subsequent years forced me to interact with fellow international students and local Japanese students in what had become my second language, and it furthered my curiosity of the world and cultivated my desire to experience it in an intimate way. The rest, as they say, is history.

I had flown around the world by the seat of my pants, often thinking more with my heart than my mind. Southeast Asia was my first big adventure. Then came a trip to Havana, Cuba, followed by a summer in India, where I spent days working at the Mother Theresa-established House of Sick and Dying and evenings interviewing and interacting with people on the streets. Next came a summer-long adventure in the Tamil region of Sri Lanka, where I worked with children who had been displaced by the war. Then, there was my trip to Saudi Arabia's neighboring country of Qatar, originally devised to follow through with a pact to reunite with an old friend but where by chance, I happened to arrive on the two-year anniversary of the U.S. invasion of Iraq. After this came a month-long adventure to Uganda to celebrate my refugee friend's brother's birthday. And the list goes on. I had little money in my bank account—just enough to get by and plan my next big adventure. I realized that if I could get beyond the "tests" the universe seemed to be challenging me with, I could feel rich. I had established meaningful connections with people across the world. I felt like my life represented a tapestry of ideas, thoughts, stories, hardships, triumphs and perspectives. As I pondered this, it became utterly clear—I needed to write a book. It would be a tangible, non-threatening way for me to introduce people who might not otherwise interact or cross paths with one another in an intentional manner, to each other. I had countless pages of hand-written notes I had taken while interviewing people and an infinite amount of pictures in boxes, bags, baskets, drawers—everywhere but photo albums. I envisioned pairing the most picturesque, touching photos with the most profound quotes I'd collected.

I started by etching out a list of the most meaningful lessons I had learned while traveling the world. Next, I sifted through my pictures to find the most ideal fit for each lesson. Then, I began combing through my articles and notes, thinking I would extract the best one-liners for each picture. Midway through, I decided I wanted more. Each quote needed context. I couldn't seem to shut off my inquisitiveness or put a moratorium on interviewing, as I kept meeting people whose stories I saw as newsworthy. I started having visions of how a particular story of a person who crossed my path could be paired with a particular lesson. And the book kept growing. I made a steadfast promise to myself that the New York Book Expo would be my official cut-off for collecting stories. But I couldn't resist. While I was at the Expo, I met a man who started publishing the Qur'an to promote interfaith alliances, I met the world's youngest author, and on the plane ride home, I sat beside a woman with roots in South Asia who happened to be a dentist and effectively scared me into tending to my teeth in spite of my fear of dentists. I had to squeeze a few more stories into my book. On my flight back to Oakland, to put the final touches on my book, I ended up sitting beside an aviation controller-in-training. This was ironic, because I had always been hyper-aware of the fact that my life depended on people like him and the fact that, in spite of my frequent traveling, I'd never overcome my fear of flying. The man shared reassuring facts and statistics about the safety of flying. I didn't exchange a business card or request a quick interview—instead, I decided to live in the moment and enjoy the conversation. I handed him a copy of *Nirvana Woman* (the magazine I write for and am managing editor of) and assured him that he would find something interesting to read for the next leg of his flight. Interestingly, on my final connecting flight home, I sat next to a woman from Texas who shared her story about losing her brother in a helicopter crash, and as a result had learned to never take any element of life for granted.

I have written and rewritten my book and expanded it so that there is no longer just one person per lesson. For better or worse, the drop-dead production deadline has approached, bringing the official journey to *The Journey of Life: 100 Lessons from Around the World* to an end. Even though I'm no longer officially collecting stories, if you end up sitting next to me on a plane, crossing paths with me in a coffeeshop or on the street, chances are we'll still have an interesting conversation and likely exchange a lesson or piece of wisdom. The most important lesson I've learned from this book project is that life really is more about the journey than the destination, more about the process than the end product, and that every single person has a story to share.

Introduction

After traveling the world for more than a decade and interviewing people from every walk of life, I have confirmed that every single person has something to offer and a lesson to teach. As I interview people in their element, I let their voices drown out all of the social ideas and stereotypes I have been exposed to. I prompt people to share a piece of themselves with me through a series of carefully crafted questions, and I am enlightened every time. I weave the human experience into articles about complex social issues, attempting to make people from all parts of the world more accessible to each other.

When I view the world through the lens of an interviewee, I watch the world break into infinite shades of gray, and the black and white vanish altogether. I am reminded that there are multiple sides to every story. I learn that people generally act with good intention, but that they are always strongly influenced by their own life experiences. It becomes nearly impossible to label anyone as entirely bad or entirely good. I learn never to sympathize and always to empathize. I learn that everyone of every religious, ethnic, national, racial and socioeconomic background, of every sexual orientation and social status, has something to teach me. My life becomes a tapestry of profound stories, unique tidbits of wisdom and memories of faces from every walk of life.

As I begin my thirtieth year of life, the world is ridden with conflict. In the midst of a war in Iraq, continual tensions in Lebanon, children still living in fear of rebels in Uganda, a reemerging ethnic conflict in Sri Lanka and a record-breaking homicide rate in Oakland, California (the city I now call home), the world feels like a crazy place. People are more afraid of each other, resentful about the past, cynical about the present and skeptical about the future. The world feels slightly off kilter. I am sad, but hopeful. I know how much I have gained by listening to people share their stories. And I know in my heart that if everyone could listen to each other, giving special attention to the voices that are sometimes not heard, the world would be a better place. I am thankful to all of the people who have crossed my path and inspired me. I feel like it is my turn to give back.

This book is a collection of the 100 most profound lessons I have gained on my journey around the world. Like life itself, this book is a combination of light hearted, fun stories and serious, trying lessons. Each lesson is intended to be as engaging as a mini-article. Each story is told in the words of the interviewee, purposefully maintaining the candor of everyday conversation. To give context, the book notes the ages of the interviewees at the time they crossed my path. Some of the people in the book are well-known figures, and others are ordinary people who live extraordinary lives. All of them speak from the heart about a profound life experience or a lesson that has changed their lives. All of them offer a lesson or a perspective that is universally applicable. This book gives us a chance to look beyond the preconceived ideas we may hold about religion, political ideology, race, class, gender and age, and focus on shared struggles and triumphs, as well as unique perspectives. It shows how much we, as humans, have to learn from each other.

Engaging in Life

Living passionately and nourishing your soul

No matter where you go or what you pursue, strive to always live with integrity.

Never lose track of who you are or what you stand for.

Sitarist Anoushka Shankar, daughter of Ravi Shankar and sister of Norah Jones, began touring when she was thirteen years old. She believes the best way to succeed as an artist is to always remember what is real and true.

"Growing up with a celebrity in my family, with fame and success around me, it was very important for me to remember that those weren't the reasons I'd be involved with music. I remember being fifteen when this really clicked for me. I was arguing with a close friend about balance—there was the musical me, the partier me, the student, the daughter and the friend. My friend pointed out that it was possible to sit on top of those worlds rather than getting absorbed. The imagery is what stuck with me. I think we have to keep remembering what matters, and keep it small and simple. It's a universal lesson and internalizing it is a gradual process. Keeping this in mind has helped me make truer choices. I resisted the crossover from classical to eclectic music for a long time, even though it would have made business sense, because I didn't feel that. I wanted to play classical music.

My album *Breathing Under Water* (which is a more eclectic, collaborative piece that I did with Karsh Kale) is a reflection of my own maturation process. I've been touring from the time I was thirteen. No matter where I am, I am always a little happy and a little sad, always have the experience of missing people, longing for people, and the album conveys that. It's about opening up as a person and a woman whose life is an inspiration of three different countries and three continents. The main impetus was trying to make a record without any boundaries. It was about being as free as I possibly could be. The older I get, the more I want my art to reflect me. Music is art and it has to be personal."

Anoushka Shankar, 26
Sitarist
New Delhi, India; San Diego, California, United States
(Originally from London, United Kingdom)

Embrace the art of vulnerability as a spiritual practice.

Letting yourself be vulnerable gives you the strength to take risks and follow your heart.

Don George loves writing and traveling. In 2001, he combined his passions and joined the *Lonely Planet* team as the global editor. In 2007, Don left *Lonely Planet* to embark on his next adventure. But he can still be found at www.donsplace.travelcollection.com.

To date, Don has traveled to more than sixty-six countries, and he says that great things have happened on every trip. Don believes that traveling has three invaluable benefits. First, it gives you perspective and teaches tolerance, respect and appreciation. Second, it teaches reciprocity. Third, it helps people connect with each other. Traveling taught Don to let himself be vulnerable. Don believes the world would be a better place if everyone took risks and let themselves be vulnerable.

"The more you open yourself up to the world, the more the world opens itself up to you. I learned early on that you can let the world control you or you can take charge of your own destiny. I've always taken risks and it's almost always worked out. Being open and letting yourself be vulnerable defuses conflict and cultivates understanding. If you take a risk and drop your defenses, it becomes contagious. The person you're interacting with is likely to do the same thing, and then you can understand each other."

Don George, 54
Former Global Editor of Lonely Planet
Piedmont, California, United States

Engage in activities you are passionate about.

Volunteer, dance, join a book club, start a new hobby or find an issue you care about and take action. No matter where in the world you are, this will help you form a community and connect with others.

3

In the 1990s, Yuko Kitagawa, a housewife from Noshiro, Japan, noticed an influx of laborers and spouses from around the world in her village. She knew that the newcomers needed access to the dominant language in order to find their niche and thrive. Yuko decided to "capture multiple butterflies with the same jar" by combining her passion for language and culture with her compassion for the growing immigrant population in her community.

"I've studied Chinese as a hobby for more than twenty years. When Chinese residents started moving to Noshiro as workers and spouses of local Japanese people, the mayor asked me to help teach Japanese. I wanted to help, so I took a year-long linguistics course at Akita University and recruited a team of volunteers. I started teaching an evening class for workers and an afternoon class for stay-at-home mothers.

People come to the class not only to learn, but also to connect with other people. In addition to class, I try to host many events recognizing Japanese and international holidays and traditions. I'm intentional about getting local Japanese and international people involved. That way, when

they see each other on the streets, they'll be more likely to at least greet each other. I want my students to feel proud of who they are and embrace their cultural backgrounds. That way when their children grow up, they can proudly say, 'I'm half this and half that.'"

Yuko Kitagawa, 58
Volunteer Language Instructor
Noshiro, Japan

17

Step out of your comfort zone whenever you can.

Most dreams cannot be realized and actualized inside our comfort zones.

Karma Gurung and John Jeffcoat have likely never crossed paths, but they have something in common. In 1993, as Karma left Nepal to start a new life in Bellevue, Washington (Seattle's neighboring city), John left Seattle to experience life in a village in Nepal. Karma went on to St. Cloud State University in Minnesota,

where he got a degree in business communication systems. Karma now dedicates all of his off hours to music. Leaving his comfort zone gave Karma the strength to find and follow his heart.

"Going somewhere to study, travel or try something new is a quest, like what Buddha did, in a way. Sometimes home is too comfortable, and if you never go away, there's no opportunity to face challenges, be on your own or grow.

My motto of life is 'Don't be a victim of circumstance, let circumstance be a victim of you.' A lot of people just take what life gives them. I've learned that if you really want something, you have to make it happen. You have to believe in the power of intentions. I've always wanted to be a musician and now I'm finally doing it. I deejay, play music and constantly try to meet and learn from other musicians. I have a nine-to-five job in a bank and spend all the rest of my time experiencing and creating music."

Karma Gurung, 30
Musician & Banker
Minneapolis, Minnesota, United States
(Originally from Manang, Nepal)

When John arrived in Nepal in 1993, his world of familiarity was turned upside down. John learned the Nepali language, culture and ways of life, as he stayed in a mud hut with his appointed host family and the family cow. The experience permanently changed John's view of the world and inspired him to use film as a means for sharing culture and promoting understanding.

"Each morning I used to wake up to the sound of a cow being milked, and then I'd get a glass of warm, sweet milk. Once, I brought some clothes to share with the villagers, and they wouldn't take them. People worried that if they took my clothes, I wouldn't have anything to wear. It was wonderful, but heart-breaking at the same time.

It's easy for people in the U.S. to be trapped in a bubble or to get into a haze of thinking this is how life should be. When taken out of your element, things that once seemed so important become frivolous. So many of the problems that exist in our lives and in the world are a result of miscommunication. If we can open our eyes a little wider, we could see that. Americans need to understand that there's a bigger world out there. I want Americans to get excited about other cultures and about the rest of the world."

John Jeffcoat, 35
Writer & Director of Outsourced
Seattle, Washington, United States

Director John Jeffcoat

Photo by Adam Weintraub

Find a creative outlet to express yourself.

Regardless of how much or little you may have, you can always find a way to share your creativity with the world.

Misao Mizuno is passionate about teaching and practicing Ancient Hula. Misao studies the traditional dance form in Hawaii and shares with students of all ages from Japan and the United States.

"We all need a creative way to express ourselves. My mission is to convey the beauty of Ancient Hula. Dancing and chanting is a prayer for all beings and a way to connect with something higher. It is a form of meditation and a way to focus on living in the present.

I start each class with a meditation chant circle to remind my students that we are all connected to the earth and to heaven. I describe the energy of the earth to remind them that we are a part of the energy circulation of nature and part of a huge universe. In the chant circle I recite an indigenous Hawaiian prayer reminding students that we live with the rhythm of Mother Earth moment by moment. Ocean waves come and go just like we breathe in and out. Energy from the earth enters your body through your feet. It goes up to the heaven via your body and head. Ancient Hula keeps me connected to myself, to earth and heaven, and reminds me to be kind to others.

Having a creative outlet, along with a sense of humor to get through the difficult times, makes life brilliant."

Misao Mizuno, 49
Ancient Hula Performer & Instructor
Big Island, Hawaii, United States
(Originally from Tokyo, Japan)

Eduardo Lopes is a percussionist, a father and a teacher. He is most passionate about rhythm and percussion. His quest to understand the borderless qualities of rhythm inspired him to develop the "just-in-time" theory, exploring the universal accessibility of rhythm. At the University of Evora in Portugal, Eduardo inspires his students to find their creative outlet in music.

"Life is a path with many crossroads and many possibilities. Music helps keep me in touch with all the possibilities of life. Like life, music is not to be understood, it is to be experienced. I created the just-in-time theory to show the globalization and universal applicability and perceptions of music. It was more like an exercise playing God in order to try to understand things that are beyond reason. The just-in-time theory shows that rhythm knows no boundaries. Life should be approached in the same way—with no boundaries, and with endless possibilities."

Eduardo Lopes, 39
Musicologist
Porto, Caiscais, Portugal

6 Use your knowledge and talents to help others.

Helping others is intrinsically and extrinsically rewarding.

The 1962 United States embargo against Cuba set an international example, making other countries hesitant to deal with Cuba and contributing to a perpetual shortage of supplies. In spite of a shortage of food, medicine and material goods, Cubans have achieved a ninety-nine percent literacy rate and trained some of the world's most talented medical practitioners. Cubans have free access to education and medical care. At any given time, there are as many as 3,000 Cuban healthcare workers helping others worldwide. Javier says that there is always a way to share and help others. These Cuban children already understand the intrinsic value of sharing. They will likely be among the next generation of volunteers.

"All people are part of the Cuban education system. We've never had a crisis of our human bodies. Our power and creativity as humans is one thing that the U.S. couldn't put a blockade on. Trying to share as human beings is more important than profit. There is no expense (in volunteering) other than the spirits and the time of the people involved. The mentality that 'I solved my problems and the rest of the people should solve theirs' is short-sighted."

Javier Duenas Oqendo, 34
Journalist & Professor at University of Havana
Havana, Cuba

Experience Bhangra.

Bhangra forces you to drop your inhibitions, live in the present and celebrate life.

Meghan Pierce was intrigued when she found a Craigslist posting online for Bhangra. She had always wanted to study Indian dance, but hesitated because she was a five-foot-eight white girl. However, once she mustered up the courage to try, she was hooked.

"Bhangra puts me in touch with the power of rhythm, energy and positive vibes. It's a non-verbal way to connect with the utmost wonderful energy. It's highly addictive, too! Hours can pass and you can find yourself jumping, boogying and shaking around while the sweat pile gathers at your feet and the calluses on your feet start to bleed, but there's no stopping the Bhangra beats!

Because of dance, I am able to express myself both verbally and non-verbally at deeper levels than ever before. I appreciate female friendships and gatherings and realize the value of the energy of a group of positive, strong women. I've overcome my shyness and love performing. In the process of learning Bhangra, I've also learned about Indian culture."

Meghan Pierce, 29
Human-Resources Manager
Vallejo, California, United States

Seek unconventional and unpractical knowledge.

You can often learn more about the world from people and real-life experiences than you can from a text book.

Zain Khandwala is a business intelligence analyst for Wells Fargo Bank by day and a student of life during off hours. Zain studies dance, music, Japanese, math and even wine. Through studying salsa, Zain has learned to love life.

"My life is a quest for knowledge and skill. It's the essence of who I am. The more I know and the more things I can do, the more people I can connect with. I learn about things that interest me and try to expand my horizons by exploring things outside of my comfort zone.

Studying salsa has given me a sense of community that I struggled to find during my twenties. It challenges me to look at things from different angles and to get beyond the normal impediments of life.

At some point linear progress stops and you need to come up with a new vantage point to tackle problems from. I've learned that nothing is really difficult. Things that seem difficult simply require patience and creativity. When something seems overwhelming, I remind myself that it just needs more time or a new lens. Life is like that—we need to keep looking at it through different lenses to get the most out of it."

Zain Khandwala, 36
Business Intelligence Consultant
Calgary, Canada
(Originally from Kuala Lumpur, Malaysia)

Through studying salsa and other genres of dance, Natalie Miske has connected with people and cultures from around the world.

"When I was a small child, I took dance lessons, but I didn't fit in with the other dancers. I still never gave up on my love for dance. As a high-school student, I wanted to take dance lessons again, but my parents only wanted me to be involved with activities that directly benefited my education, so I had to be strategic. I had to make my love for dance educational.

I enrolled in Spanish class and convinced my parents that salsa lessons would help me understand the cultural aspects of Spanish. I took a salsa dance class and the rest is history. I kept taking different types of dance classes and eventually became a dance major in college.

You can dance with people who have different beliefs, ideologies, religions, cultures and languages than you. Dance is a way for people to come together and connect with each other. As an American, I sometimes feel like I don't have any culture. My roots are Italian, German and Hungarian, but I don't know anything about the experiences of those cultures. Studying dance allows me to learn about other cultures through the music, the moves and the instructor. Dancing keeps me in the present."

Natalie Miske, 24
Advocate for the Arts
Los Angeles, California, United States

Develop a weekly ritual with your friends.

Everyone needs a group of friends to exchange silly stories with and to dream, laugh and connect with. It's good for the mind, body and soul.

These ladies begin their weekly ritual at 9:30 every Saturday morning at Bhangra class to partake in their shared passion of dance, and continue at an Indian chaat house (snack shop), where they indulge in their other passions—aloo parathas (Indian potato pancakes) and endless cups of chai, at their very own picnic in the parking lot. Their lives are richer because of this ritual.

"No matter what my week was like, whether it was good or bad, I know that come Saturday morning, I will be surrounded by people who I truly love and have truly impacted my life. It's the perfect way to end the week and even a more perfect way to start the weekend. It doesn't matter what is said or what isn't said— we all know that we are there, not only for the food and chai, but for each other. We're there not because we have to be, but because we want to be there out of our friendship, respect and love for each other."

Carrie Kroon, 27
Office Manager
Oakland, California, United States
(Originally from Fairmount, Minnesota)

"On Saturday mornings, I heal, reflect and rejoice. Bhangra class rejuvenates my body. Our breakfast at the chaat shop gives me the chance to laugh and rejuvenate my mind and soul. It proves time and time again how lucky I am to have friends in my life to laugh, cry, eat, drink, dance and solve the world's problems with. It may seem insignificant to others who have not experienced the healing powers of a ritual with friends, but it is an important part of my life."

Suman Raj-Grewal, 41
Bank Manager
Hercules, California, United States
(Originally from Lautoka, Fiji)

"It's a time when happiness, laughter, love, smiles, frustrations, sadness, even pain, are shared without judgment or hesitation. It's 'Soul's Sunday,' a time of healing and nourishment, a time of letting go and connecting with something bigger than just yourself. For us, it's like going to a rock concert and participating in a spiritual retreat all at the same time. Regardless of what else is going on in the world or in our own lives, for those couple of hours, everything is just the way it's supposed to be. Through our conversations, we travel the world and beyond and come back richer with knowledge, experience, humility, lots of love and, best of all, humor of its own kind. It's a priceless gift and a reminder of how truly beautiful life is."

Vicki Virk, 33
Dancer
San Francisco, California, United States
(Originally from Punjab, India)

Don't let wounds from the past paralyze you in the present.

Rather than being resentful about the hardships you've faced in the past, be determined to do better next time.

It took Willy Ann Heisler four years to leave her abusive relationship. When she finally left, she found herself again and rediscovered love.

"I think of this like a snake that keeps shedding its skin and starting over with new, fresh skin. The old skin is no longer functional or necessary. In order to grow, we need to shed our old skin to move on and replace it with the new.

I was stuck in a pattern of trying to be the caretaker, the helper and the one to 'save' others. I had lived in fear, lost touch, distanced myself from friends and no longer recognized myself. It took me four years to leave, but now I look at the relationship as a learning experience. I needed to learn lessons to grow. Leaving gave me the chance to reassess what a healthy relationship was, decide what I would like to tolerate and what was unacceptable. I had to pull up my self-esteem and rediscover myself.

It was affirming when I met the man who is now my husband. When I met him, I remember thinking that he had so many qualities I hoped and prayed for in a companion. I realized that God does listen. It might take a while, but your wishes will be granted—and that is affirming. I feel like I have no other choice but to love. Loving people is easy. If I did not have love in my heart for people, I would have a very empty feeling inside— and who wants to feel empty?"

Willy Ann Heisler, 30
Native-American Social Worker
Ogema, Minnesota, United States

Approach life as a checkerboard, not a ladder.

Rather than worrying about climbing to the top, let yourself experience everything your heart desires.

When Mike Zoll was a senior in college, he spotted a poster that looked like a checkerboard with people from all over the world, bearing the slogan "Discover the World: Semester at Sea." He was intrigued by the idea of getting a cross-sectional view of the world through an old means of transportation—a ship. While on the global adventure, Mike learned to live life as a journey not a destination, and to approach life as a checkerboard, not a ladder.

"When I turned twenty-nine, I went on a 100-day voyage around the world. I visited Turkey, Russia, Egypt, India, Malaysia, Taiwan, Japan and Hong Kong. I loved the culture of each place and the beauty of the people. India is the country that most knocked me off my axis of familiarity. I was amazed by people's ability to be satisfied with their place in life, regardless of how poor they were.

The experience made me appreciate difference and travel. It made me love the 'Semester at Sea' program. In May 2006, I made the difficult decision to leave my position as the vice provost at a small Catholic college in California to accept a position with Semester at Sea. Accepting the position meant moving my family cross-country and taking a slight pay cut. It didn't necessarily make practical sense from a career point of view. But it embodied what I was most passionate about. I thought long and hard and discussed all the variables with my wife. We knew it was the right thing to do.

Life is a journey, not a destination. A ladder is like the destination. A checkerboard is the journey. When you approach life that way, you might take a diagonal step downwards. But when it comes down to it, it's all about following your heart, having a zest for life and doing what you are most passionate about. If you follow your heart, you can't go wrong."

Mike Zoll, 46
Dean of Student Services, Semester at Sea
Charlottesville, Virginia, United States

29

12 Take risks.

Choose spontaneity over practicality whenever possible.

Yukiko Yoda led a fairly comfortable life in Japan, where she had a stable job and an established community of friends. When she approached thirty, she left Japan to attend a residential undergraduate college in the United States without a firm grasp of English. Taking that risk is the best thing that Yukiko has ever done.

"Moving to the U.S. to be a student meant leaving behind a stable job that I had worked at for nearly a decade, (as well as) leaving my friends, my mother, my grandmother and a very comfortable life in Tokyo. In the context of a foreign place where I did not speak the language well, I struggled to understand the meaning of life my place in the world, and my identity as a person. I sometimes wondered if I had made the right decision. Now I realize that this is what I had to do to discover new and amazing aspects of the world, and of me. I know that the biggest risk I could have taken would have been to stay in my comfort zone rather than following my heart. I am a better person because I took a risk."

Yukiko Yoda, 32
Expatriate Consultant
Tokyo, Japan

Take public transportation.

It is better for the environment and keeps you in touch with people from all walks of life.

13

Saqib Mousoof makes ends meet as an information-technology engineer at Ask.com. He spends all of his spare time following his passions—writing, developing film scripts and traveling. Saqib is working on his first film, *Kala Pul—The Black Bridge*, based in his hometown, Karachi, Pakistan.

"I take public transportation every day. Rather than being stressed with traffic, I can read a book or just kick back. But my favorite thing about taking public transportation is that it puts me in the middle of the human experience. Unlike being stuck in your car in a traffic jam, the train is communal. You are at one with everyone on the train and get an opportunity to see all kinds of people who make life real."

Saqib Mousoof, 36
Information Technology Engineer & Writer
San Francisco, California, United States
(Originally from Karachi, Pakistan)

31

Embrace the unpredictability of life.

If we always knew what was coming next, life would be far less interesting.

Yen Sang Mak left Malaysia with a clear plan for what she wanted to accomplish in life. Through a series of events, Yen Sang has learned that life doesn't always go as planned.

"Although we want everything in life to be in our control, a lot of things aren't. At some point, fate takes over. Sometimes you just have to choose to live with the situations that are challenging you the most and try to stay positive and optimistic. When I was in school, I tried to plan my life. I wanted to get a green card so I could work in the United States. Now, I know that there's no point in thinking and planning so far ahead, when everything in life changes so much over time. A lot of people my age are married with kids. I thought I would be married by now too, but I'm not. I choose not to get stressed with the ideas of the older generation or be influenced by what society thinks. Other people tell me they are amazed by how comfortable I am with being single. They are amazed with my ability to live life to the utmost."

Yen Sang Mak, 31
Sales Manager
Ipoh, Perak, Malaysia

Never let yourself be a victim of circumstance.

Instead, make the best of your circumstances.

15

This motto belongs to Karma Gurung from Nepal. Although Karma has never met Shingo Watanabe from Japan, his life motto is the perfect summation of Shingo's life experience.

"Throughout my life, I felt like I didn't have choices. Everything was decided for me based on circumstances. I took eight entrance exams for college and passed only the one for Akita University, my last choice. I wanted to become a doctor, but was only accepted to do the chemistry track. Rather than being resentful, I decided to focus on being happy in the realm I was in. When I told my advisor in Japan I wanted to transfer to medical school, he laughed at me. Without his approval, I couldn't do that in the Japanese education system. So I had to focus on what I could do.

I decided to try and go to the U.S. for graduate school. After I found a program that I liked at Penn State, I tried contacting the advisor dozens of times and heard nothing. Finally, I showed up at Penn State with no appointment and found the advisor. I applied, but didn't hear back for months. I wrote one last e-mail letting the advisor know that I was prepared for rejection or acceptance, but needed an answer. That day I got an e-mail saying that I had been accepted. I was assigned to do research on something that I

didn't want to do, but I did it anyway. While doing the research, I tested one idea that I had, and it turned out to be the most efficient solution. In the process of doing something that I didn't want to do and making the best of it, I came up with original research.

The moral of my story is: keep doing what you're best at. If you have only one option, go for it, because it will end up being the best choice for you. I'm not a medical doctor, but soon I'll have a doctorate in chemistry. I'll go on to find a job that's satisfying to me, get married, have lots of kids and live near the ocean."

Shingo Watanabe, 29
Chemistry Graduate Student
University Park, Pennsylvania, United States
(Originally from Noshiro, Japan)

33

16 Imagine the world through the eyes of children.

Spend time with children. Listen to them and learn from them. They are the hope for the future.

Zoe doesn't yet fully understand the complexities of issues like homelessness and poverty, but she's already developed a sense of compassion. Imagine what the world would be like if we all saw the world through Zoe's eyes.

"If someone doesn't have lunch, you can share with them. Otherwise, they'll get hungry and they might need to wait a long time. I always try to share. Today I shared my Cheetos (with my dad's co-workers). If you see someone who doesn't have a home, maybe you can invite them to stay at your house, until their house is ready."

Zoe, 6
First Grader
Fremont, California, United States

John Silliphant imagined the world through the eyes of children when he launched an international peace initiative. By empowering children on both sides of the Indian-Pakistani border to connect with each other through letters, John hopes to inspire Indian and Pakistani children to see each other as friends, not enemies. He hopes adults from throughout the world will be inspired to follow the example of the youngest members of society.

"I started working on Friends Without Borders and collected tens of thousands of heart-to-heart letters written between the children of India and Pakistan. The idea is really simple. Children have a natural tendency toward openness and friendship. By tapping into this inherent goodwill and capturing it in a letter, these letters carry with them the warm feelings that help to build lasting friendships. My hope is that these genuine messages can work to counteract the effects of the false stereotypes and prejudices that many of these kids would otherwise inherit. And who knows? Perhaps these new seeds of friendship may one day blossom into a more peaceful world as this generation matures."

John Silliphant, 37
Founder, Friends Without Borders
Old Greenwich, Connecticut, United States

17 Love unconditionally and without fear.

Sparks will come and go, but love is ultimately a choice. Choosing to love is choosing to be vulnerable. Choosing to let others be vulnerable is choosing to love. Love is knowing someone's flaws and weaknesses, but focusing on their strengths.

Photo by Collin Krauthamer

When it came time for Shib Sah, a math teacher from Janakpur, Nepal, to marry, he was introduced to many prospective wives. But he fell for one unique woman, Ranjana. She was resilient and strong, and happened to have only one breast, as the result of a birth defect.

"I didn't care about what Ranjana had or didn't have. I loved her heart. I loved the way she behaved and interacted with other people. My family didn't care that Ranjana had only one real breast, because I didn't care. If Ranjana married another man (who might not have been able to get past her birth defect), there might have been trouble—she might have been abused. Love is deep. Suppose that after marriage one person gets sick or becomes disabled—the amount of love you have shouldn't decrease, it should become stronger."

Shib Sah, 37
Cashier
Davis, California, United States
(Originally from Janakpur, Nepal)

Jeremy Splinter became friends with a woman from a very different background than his. Without knowing it, Tricia inspired Jeremy to see the endless possibilities of love. Jeremy pursued Tricia and waited patiently. Today, Tricia is Jeremy's best friend and life partner.

"I always had my defenses up and was skeptical of love. When I met my partner, I forgot about all that. I knew there was something unique about her. We struggled a lot for our first five months, because I was more ready for love than she was. But I didn't give up.

When you know something is right, you have to be willing to fight for it, and that's what I did. Patience is the most important thing. You have to let love happen, by trusting yourself to make the right decisions in your life.

Tricia has been through a lot in her life. When I met her, I knew she was different. To draw a parallel, it was like seeing an average rock with a sparkling diamond on the inside. She was wearing boy jeans, a loose-fitting t-shirt and had her hair pulled back in a ponytail, but I knew she was amazing. Some shallow guys might have overlooked her along the way, but I knew there was something deep and special about her, and I never gave up. Now, she's a well-polished diamond. She has confidence and she is determined. She is a successful teacher, and I know she will go far in life. She wears clothes that represent her. She is a diamond both on the inside and outside. That is why I love her."

Jeremy Splinter, 32
Home Inspector
Stevens Point, Wisconsin, United States

37

18 Be inquisitive.

Ask open-ended, nonjudgmental questions. Asking questions gives others the opportunity to share a piece of their life story. It helps them know that they are valued as human beings and gives you the opportunity to learn.

I gained a reputation as the one who asked too many questions as a young child. I was curious about everything. I loved to ask questions as much as I loved to write in my journal. I loved the thought of being able to ask questions for a living. This inspired me to become a journalist.

Each time I interview someone about their life story, I am enlightened and rewarded when the interviewee discovers a new part of himself or herself.

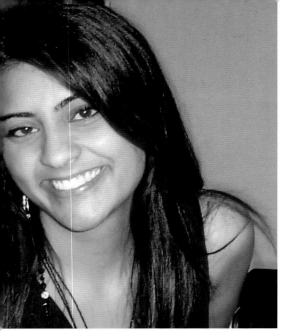

In looking for individuals who valued inquisitively as much as me, I had no choice but to reach out to my journalist friends. I have yet to meet a journalist who is not addicted to asking questions. Rupa Dev and Tom LaVenture may be journalists of different generations, but both love that wearing their "journalist hats," gives them license to ask endless questions.

"When I first started telling people I wanted to be a journalist, most people responded with skepticism and some were downright discouraging. Everybody pointed out the long hours,

small salary, dangerous travel and stressful deadlines—endless reasons not to pursue the path. In college, I took the advice to heart and began bouncing from one major to the next in hopes of finding a more practical career replacement. But no matter how far away I tried to go, I found myself always getting reeled back into the field because of my inherently inquisitive nature. When I would attend an event for fun, like an open-mic performance put on by rising South Asian hip-hop artists, I had an itching urge to ask questions about everything; I wanted to learn about their lives, work and love for the music they produced. The more questions I asked, the more I realized just how misunderstood these hip-hop artists were within my own community. Their compelling story, alongside those of many others, just hadn't been heard or told yet.

I couldn't overcome my thirst for hearing and sharing others' stories. Shifting gears to transition back into journalism wasn't a conscious decision on my part. Sometimes, you don't choose your life and career path; instead, it chooses you. If I didn't find a way to write these stories, they may not have been told. And that, I believe, would be a serious loss to humanity. To be inquisitive makes life interesting; a once-stranger may now be your best friend, an organization you were intrigued by now may be your current employer. I've learned that if you ask enough questions, not necessarily because it's your job, but because you have a sincere interest in the subject that you are covering, it's possible to connect with almost anyone. To achieve such human connectivity is truly a gift."

Rupa Dev, 21
Journalist & College Student
Urbana-Champaign, Illinois, United States

"I was always reminded growing up that 'the only dumb question is the question not asked.' Yet all too often, I would avoid asking the question that might reveal ignorance, annoy or at worst prolong a class or interview by inviting a lecture. I have learned that research and preparation does not diminish inquisitiveness; it only broadens and deepens the scope of understanding, and raises even more thoughtful and enlightened questions. In my experience, asking the obvious questions with an anticipated reply often brings the most unexpected and revealing response.

Sensitivity and awareness allows for tolerance within our own paradigm. But to grow more fully, we need to have direct interaction with people from communities other that our own. We can study the history and common suffer-ing of a group of people. But by meeting a person of that culture and questioning their experience directly, we can gain a foundation of understanding and familiarity that will dismiss our misconceptions."

Tom LaVenture, 43
Editor of Asian American Press
Inner Grove Heights, Minnesota, United States
(Originally from New Richmond, Wisconsin)

19 Communicate with strangers.

Whether it's the person sitting next to you in a coffeeshop or the person driving your cab, everyone has something to teach you. Meeting and befriending people who are raised in different social environments with different ideologies and ways of seeing the world gives us the chance to adopt new perspectives.

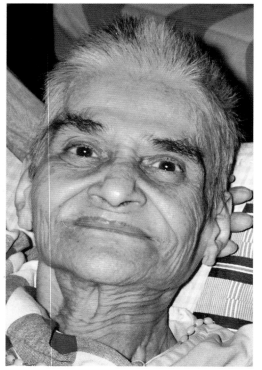

Marie asked me to paint her nails. Although her body was decaying to the point that her bony frame was visible beneath a thin layer of skin, her mind and memory were very keen. Tucked under her pillow I found an Aries horoscope book. Marie told me that her birthday was on March 24th and she was dying to read her book, but that she couldn't because she was half blind without her glasses. The fact that Marie and I shared the Aries sign piqued my interest. I looked up our horoscope for the day and began chatting with her. Soon, she became my friend and my reason for returning to work every day, as well as my inspiration to stay in India. My life is better because I talked to this stranger. It is richer every time I talk to any strangers.

In memory of Marie, 85
Former Patient at Prem Dan
Calcutta, India

Drivers have seen a little bit of every-thing, met more people than the aver-age person will ever meet and almost always have an intriguing story to share.

I have never met an uninteresting taxi, rickshaw or company driver. Many of the drivers I've encountered are educated, well traveled and intricately aware of the realities of our world. They are in touch with people at all levels of society, as their jobs and lives depend on it.

I met Harry Singh, an expatriate from Punjab, India, while visiting a friend in Doha, Qatar. Harry had been working in the Middle East to support his fam-ily in India for more than a decade. He had a distinct laugh and a unique smell. Although Harry and I didn't speak a common language, we under-stood common gestures, the universal power of laughing and our common love for food. On Fridays—Qatar's "Sunday" and Harry's day off—Harry treated me to aloo perathas from his expatriate friend's shop.

Inspired by Harry Singh, 60
Driver
Doha, Qatar
(Originally from Punjab, India)

Do what you can to make the world a better place.

Never let the inhibitions of others stop you from making a difference.

Jang-wan Kim would have done anything to go to India. When she was unsuccessful with convincing her parents to let her go, she came up with an alternative plan.

"I wanted to do something more valuable than traveling and visiting famous places. I really wanted to go to India and volunteer, but my family thought of it as a dirty, poor place with mosquitoes and malaria everywhere. They also knew about the travel advisory that was in place at the time, asking all foreigners to leave because of the tension between India and Pakistan about

Kashmir. I didn't want my family to worry, so I told them I would go to England instead. A month after I arrived, I wrote a letter to my sister telling her where I really was and describing some of my experiences. My parents saw the letter and found out I was in India. At first, they were worried and really wanted me to come home. Now they have given up, because I am here and there is nothing they can do.

Volunteering in India makes me feel very connected to the people. I started out in Orissa working for a social-development organization and planned to stay six months. Now, I've been here more than one year. I've gone to Bangladesh twice to renew my visa. I don't know where I'll go next, but for right now I am working at Prem Dan (the Mother Theresa House for the sick and dying). I feel lucky when I'm there, because I speak some Bengali and can communicate with the patients. When they ask for my help, I feel valuable. It's nice that we can rely on each other. I can't speak perfectly, but I can communicate in two dialects. I hope I can learn Hindi someday."

Jang-wan Kim, 24
Volunteer
Seoul, Korea

Mobilizing, Mentoring & Motivating

Inspiring others and setting an example

Think and act outside the box.
Connect with your roots through music or art, and share with others.

Robin Sukhadia inspires children around the world to think and act outside the box and envision new possibilities in life with the tabla drums.

"My dad always had Indian music playing in the house as I was growing up. I didn't know much about it, but I thought it sounded amazing. When I turned twenty-two, I went to India for my first time with a study-abroad program. That is when I took my first tabla lesson. It was my first experience studying an instrument not based on the Western tradition. There was nothing written down for me to follow. There was a particular way to sit, to breathe, to show respect to the teacher, to concentrate, to use the instrument as a meditative tool and to listen to the sound. The whole thing was very mysterious. I knew that by learning tabla, I could learn more about my roots and my culture than I could ever learn by reading a book. I developed a love for tabla that inspired me to take many years of lessons and to pursue an MFA in world music.

Most people don't know that the tabla, one of the most beautiful-sounding instruments in the world, comes from Afghanistan. Our society has been programmed to think of Afghanistan as a wasteland of people that can be dismissed. Most people don't know how rich the culture of that country is. It's amazing to watch culture evolve and boundaries resolve. At one time, tabla was reserved only for the most elite members of society. Now, the drums have cut through all boundaries—socioeconomic, cultural and geographic.

I use the tabla to get others to think outside the box. I teach tabla to at-risk kids around the world. I work with poor kids in Calcutta, kids who have grown up in the midst of religious conflict in Gujarat and juvenile delinquents in Colorado. The children in India learn to concentrate better. Hindu and Muslim children learn how to create music together and become friends in the process. Teens in Colorado gain life-coping skills and learn to appreciate a new culture. It's amazing to create beautiful compositions with my students."

Robin Sukhadia, 31
Tabla Artist & Instructor, Project Ahimsa
San Francisco, California, United States
(Originally from India)

46

Mobilize, mentor and motivate.

Rather than giving definitive answers, micromanaging or offering your prescribed solution to fix a problem, inspire others to look within. The answers to life's most difficult questions are inside us.

Vicki Virk is a living testament to this philosophy. Vicki moved from Punjab, India to California when she was twelve years old. In finding her path to dance, she went from being a high school student that didn't quite fit in, to a business graduate from Fresno State University, to an investment banker, to a woman with all the markings of an attorney. But Vicki believed the universe had a different plan for her. She traveled, meditated and realized she was meant to dance and teach others to dance.

"One day I wrote the quote, 'Move to the rhythm of your soul and you'll never miss a beat.' I am not sure what drove me to write that quote, but I do believe the quote has inspired every decision I've made since. I knew I had to find what it was that drove me. I was on a quest to figure out what I was meant to do. Every day I prayed and asked for guidance from the universe or a sign. Then it came.

One day I was driving to San Francisco and listening to Bhangra music, and suddenly a light bulb went off as I thought out loud how great it would be to share this beautiful dance and music with people of all backgrounds. I started teaching Bhangra the very next week. I began with two students in an old, run-down studio and the rest is history. I now teach Bhangra all over the San Francisco Bay Area and perform with my very own dance troupe.

Sharing my love of dance with others is a dream come true. Every day I meet someone new, learn something new, dance with someone new—

what could be better!? Dancing is like celebrating life. It doesn't matter what you do or how you do it; it's about having a zest for life.

When I teach Bhangra, I tell my students to dance like no one is watching and to incorporate that energy when they are learning the dance. I teach them that the best way to learn to dance is to keep trying. Instead of correcting students each time they do a move, I let them keep trying in their own way while I continue teaching the dance form. Eventually, they get comfortable, become confident and improve.

I think that what my students learn on the dance floor transfers to their lives outside of class. It teaches students to live life in a way that is most true to them. It teaches them to keep trying even when life seems difficult and to keep an open mind toward new and unfamiliar things."

Vicki Virk, 33
Dancer
San Francisco, California, United States
(Originally from Punjab, India)

Be willing to change.

Rather than expecting life to adapt to you, adapt to life.

Joanna Snawder moved from Louisville, Kentucky to the San Francisco Bay Area in 1995 to complete her college education at Mills College. Today, Joanna considers Oakland home. In her profession, as a sexual assault awareness coordinator at Saint Mary's College of California, she inspires young women and men to be open to change.

"If you always do what you've always done, you'll always have what you've always had. I heard this a few years ago and have tried to keep it in mind ever since. I try to remind myself of this when I find myself repeating unhealthy habits. It helps me be open to new experiences. It gives me the courage to try new restaurants, visit new places and make new friends. It's so simple, but it helps to have the philosophy spelled out in a tangible way so I can really apply it."

Joanna Snawder, 32
Sexual Assault Awareness Coordinator
Oakland, California, United States
(Originally from Louisville, Kentucky)

No matter what you do in life, vow to always have fun.

Do what you love, be determined and you will succeed.

John Zabala put this philosophy into practice when deciding what to major in, what to do after graduation and what advice to offer other college students.

"When I worked with incoming freshmen at college orientation, lots of students asked me what they should major in. I told them they should major in whatever they thought would be the most fun. If you're not having fun with what you're doing, you'll just be going through the motions of life.

I really enjoyed being involved with college as an orientation advisor and as the president of the student body. My experience at college encompassed so many different experiences and people that have influenced my life positively. When it came time to graduate and decide on a career, it was easy for me. What I loved most was learning and working with students. Why not get paid for doing what I love? I applied for graduate school at the New School for Social Research and will get my Master's of Arts in Liberal Studies. Maybe that will lead me to being a professor, maybe not. But I'll have fun and grow in the process of trying."

John Zabala, 22
Graduate Student
New York City, New York, United States
(Originally from Los Angeles, California)

25

Never forget where you came from or who inspired you along the way.

The people you've encountered throughout life have made you who you are today.

As a driver for a wealthy expatriate family, Faiz Salim Shriff Sale feels trapped. He dreams of working in media, but doesn't have the financial means to pursue an education. Yet Faiz promises that when he does succeed, he will never forget his roots.

"We are friends now because we are both struggling. If one of us gets rich, we might not talk to each other anymore. It shouldn't be that way. No matter how much money you have, you should not forget where you came from. You should never start to think that you are better than others because you have more than they do. If you do well, go back and help others behind you.

Most of the rich people in Uganda are expatriates. If you want to have money in this country and you are black, you have to work hard, twenty-four hours a day, seven days a week. I am educated and I have a diploma, but being a driver is the best job I can get in this country. I want to go abroad and study mass communication, but I don't have enough money in my bank account to get a visa. I don't think I can get ahead in this society, because the money I earn is barely enough to cover food. But if I ever do get ahead, I will go back and help others."

Faiz Salim Shriff Sale, 24
Driver
Kampala, Uganda

Sanjib Kumar Sah comes from a family of merchants in Janakpur, Nepal. Although Sanjib is successful as an entrepreneur, a developer, an engineer and an artist in his spare time, he vows never to forget his humble beginnings or all of the people who have inspired him along the way.

"I remember being a pretty happy kid growing up in Nepal. My brothers and I would play games that we learned about in the Ramayana, and make bows and arrows out of bamboo shoots. I ran around all the time and never wore shoes. On my first day of school, I showed up in flip-flops and my teacher sent me home. I had to wear my dad's oversized shoes that day because I didn't own close-toed shoes. I became friends with my family's helper. He used to find old shoeboxes, scrap paper, anything he could draw on. He would draw amazing pictures of mythical figures from our religion (Hinduism). He was also a sculptor. I used to find his creations lying around and I would try to

copy them. I sometimes went to visit him in the little shack he stayed in, so he could teach me how to draw. That's what made me love to draw and paint.

When I was eight, I remember taking a long journey with my family. I had no concept of

53

where we were going. First, we were on a rickshaw, then we were on a bus, then a train, then a plane and then I was in Japan, eating ice cream for my first time. We landed in San Francisco and took a tour. California was going to be my new home.

When I got to school in Davis to Mrs. Luddington's classroom, it was show-and-tell day. I remember being impressed with how grown-up all the students were. I didn't know any English, so I used to get sent to the library to watch *Sesame Street* every day for the first few months. Looking back, I think my years in elementary school were the best years of my life. At that age, no one cares what you look like or if you're different.

In junior high, people let me know I was different. I would sometimes get called names. Everyone grew and they were all a lot taller than me. I knew I was foreign, tiny compared to everyone else and didn't think I was good-looking. I didn't really feel like I belonged. But I was pretty resilient and determined to overcome my social obstacles. I learned to be resourceful. I would find one occasional outfit on the sale rack and convince my parents to buy it. I would set goals for myself. I started playing sports and developed a social life.

In retrospect, I think this helped me create a sense of balance for myself and has given me the skill set to relate to almost any kind of person. If I could do anything differently, I would have spent less time worrying about fitting in with the 'in' crowd and more time with the people who were less concerned about status and were willing to accept others as they were.

Someday, I would like my kids to have the chance to learn about my culture, and I would like to learn with them. At the same time, I am a constant believer in evolution. You make your culture what it is. I think it will be great when culture is a total mix and a blending of many different types of people. This will make the world more accessible to everyone."

Sanjib Kumar Sah, 33
Developer & Engineer
West Hollywood, California, United States
(Originally from Janakpur, Nepal)

Be positive.

Positive energy is contagious, negative energy consumes you.

26

Fernando Garcia is one of eight children. Fernando's parents, farmers by trade, took up extra jobs selling chips, fruit and cookies in an effort to save up enough money to fund a community-college education for Fernando and his brother. Watching his parents struggle inspired Fernando to make a life-changing decision. He left Mexico and is paving his path in the United States. He credits positivism as his source of strength.

"One day, when I was riding the bus to class, I looked out the window and saw my dad. He was on his way to work, carrying a big cooler and two bikes. Seeing him work so hard made my blood boil.

At that moment, I knew I needed to go to the U.S. to try and better our lives. I moved to Bakersfield, California, and started out working in a field, earning $5.25 an hour. I sent $125 to my family each week. Next, I got a job in a packing company and worked my way up to a manager position. I got involved with the church in the community and met my wife while I was singing in the choir. After we got married, my wife and I moved to Lafayette, California so my wife could finish college. I am happy to be living here. I have worked really hard for everything I have, so I am very proud of myself. I've learned the power of believing in yourself and your ideas. When you open your heart to learning, you can find sincerity, love and peace.

I'm working in a café now, and studying to become a teacher. I love teaching. When I work with the children's choir at my church, I love hearing the children sing. They sing with all their hearts. Children are real, sincere and happy. I get a heavy feeling in my heart from working with them and I want to be a positive influence. I feel like a kid at heart."

Fernando Garcia, 28
Server & Aspiring Teacher
Lafayette, California, United States
(Originally from Guanajuato, Mexico)

27 Be introspective.

Reflecting on your stake in life's events gives you invaluable perspective.

Nancy Glenn reflects on her strengths and weaknesses as a mother, a wife, a psychologist and as a human being each year between Rosh Hashanah and Yom Kippur.

"There are times during the year that are devoted to reflection within the Jewish tradition. Each year, during the ten-day period of reflection—beginning with Rosh Hashanah, the Jewish New Year, and culminating with Yom Kippur, the Day of Atonement—referred to as the high holy days, I reflect on life. This is a time for introspection, a time to review the past year—our successes and our mistakes. It's a time to stop, sit back and think, take stock and plan personal changes to make in the New Year.

I think about this in regard to the important relationships in my life as a mother, a spouse, a friend, and in my role as a psychologist at a college. I reflect on the connections that I try to make with others. I think about ways I hoped to reach a particular student, but couldn't. I think of important moments when I tried to reach my kids, but was unsuccessful. I reflect on the ways that I communicated with others. I try to understand what was happening in my life—what was happening within myself that kept me from reaching another, from communicating what I had hoped. I think about what I can do differently in the coming year and reflect on what I am willing to do.

I consider a life without time for reflection and introspection somewhat of an empty life. Reflection helps me feel grounded, gives me perspective and allows time for forgiveness of my own actions and acceptance of my humanity."

Nancy Glenn, 48
Psychologist
San Francisco, California, United States

Be a role model.
Live your ideologies and respect the ideologies of others.

28

Ishvinder Bassi is guided by Sikhism to be a positive role model for her children.

"I practice Sikhism by going to the Gurudwara every Sunday. Every time I go, I learn something new. I am regularly reminded to help the needy, and I feel some kind of peace and happiness doing that. Apart from that, I have a little prayer corner in my apartment where my kids and I pray and light incense sticks. When my kids need something, they go and pray for it. When my kids see me praying and having faith in God, they too, start to believe. That itself is a great gain as a mother. My daughter knows that at times when I am upset, I spend time in my prayer corner talking it out. Sikhism teaches women that it is up to us to teach the ways of life to the kids, and I am trying to do that. I think being a woman in itself is life's biggest reward, as we get to give life to others.

In our religion, we have a saying: 'Jo bole so nihal.' And everyone replies: 'Sat sri akal.' I can't translate the slogan, but I get goosebumps just thinking about it. There is so much power in it. Sometimes there is so much noise at our gatherings, and it seems like no one listens to anyone. As soon as someone shouts the slogan, everything gets quiet and peaceful, and that indeed is powerful."

Ishvinder Bassi, 37
Nurse
Kisumu, Kenya

57

29 Be eclectic.

Be intentional about integrating different types of food, fashion, music and ideas into your life.

Kush Arora embarked on a life of music as a young child. He started out as a pianist, and traded his piano for a drum kit by the time he was nine years old. Kush began experimenting with computers and mixing equipment soon after, and ever since he's been hooked. Kush is addicted to music and loves pushing people to conceptualize a borderless world through his music.

"We live in a world where we are totally tied together and dependent on each other. The more people anywhere expose themselves to different cultural elements, the better off they always are— they are, as a result, more aware, empowered and educated. Music is the easiest way people of different cultures can find out about each other. The last thing I expect people to do is pick up a book and read (about a faraway country). I haven't actually deeply studied any culture academically. Instead, I've learned through observation and interacting with folks. Countries are always blending into one another and influencing each other. When the commonalities go unnoticed, racism and sterile lifestyles prevail and very few things change. It takes something both groups like to bring them together—like food, art, music. Moreover, it's so boring to just be around the culture or folks you grew up with.

Sometimes I want my music to make people aware of the lifeblood this world has right now, and how tense it is. There are many layers in my music, because I want people to see the many layers of the issues they are dealing with. Sometimes I want to make people happy and encourage them to let go of their pain, as I send them on a journey through instruments or vocals. I hope my music inspires people to shape their lives in a way that is free from boundaries. I want it to encourage people to think for themselves in a world where depth and beauty are not always simultaneously available."

Kush Arora, 25
Producer & Musician
San Leandro, California, United States

30

If there is no path leading you where you'd like to go, create your own.

The most amazing things in life are often not on the paved path.

Maria Eugenia Arrezola-Clark left Mexico when she was pregnant with her daughter, Elia, in search of a better life. Inspired by her mom's resiliency, Elia was the first member of her extended family to attend college and get a master's degree.

"I was born in Mexico. My mother raised my three sisters, two brothers and me, while my father worked in the United States. There was no bus, so I used to walk far to get to school every day. I studied at the Seguro Social Familiar to learn how to cook, bake and sew clothes. After my sisters were born, my family decided to go to California. I got my first job at a tomato factory. The next season I worked in the field, and then I worked as a cook at a camp for immigrant children and workers. After that I did in-home health care. In 1979 I went to a school for adult education so I could get my GED. Soon after, I went back to Mexico.

In 1981 my daughter Elia was born. I was an unwed mother and I didn't have a career. I didn't think we would make it in Mexico, so I brought Elia to the U.S. I used to dream of becoming a nurse. That didn't happen, but I did get a job in a nursing home, where I have been working for the past twenty-three years. What I am most proud of is my daughter Elia. I love her. She has something I will never have. She went to school so she could have a career of her own. She got her master's degree in May 2006. Now she is creating her own life and living her dream. If we stayed in Mexico, she wouldn't have had the chance to accomplish this. I became a citizen of this country in 1990, and I am so proud to be here with my daughter.

Maria Eugenia Arrezola-Clark, 54
Nursing Assistant
Woodland, California, United States
(Originally from Mexico)

"My mom always told me to educate myself, because she didn't get the chance to educate herself in Mexico. She broke the mold in our culture. She became pregnant with me when she was twenty-nine years old and unmarried. After I was born, she packed her bags and me, and moved to the U.S. to start a new life.

My mom and her sisters all came here in hopes of bettering future generations, but it has been challenging. My aunts didn't have the chance to make it past high school. Many of my cousins got involved in gangs and drugs and ended up dropping out of high school. They all had kids at a young age. I want to be there for my cousins' children, to mentor them and set an example for them.

I was able to go to college and finish my master's degree. I have worked hard to get where I am today. I am determined to succeed, and when I do, I will not forget where I came from or who helped me along the way. I am bettering myself, and by bettering myself, I will better my people. By always remembering where I came from, by giving back to my community, and by mentoring those students who will continue the path of higher education, I will break the cycle."

Elia Moreno, 24
Intercultural Center Coordinator
Woodland, California, United States
(Originally from Mexico)

Inspire and be inspired.

Let yourself be inspired by anything and anyone at any time. Do what you can to inspire others.

Nubia Leonor Filice never had the opportunity to attend college or pursue her dream career. But she has mastered something that even the most educated people often never master. Nubia has an innate ability to appreciate and find happiness in the simplest things in life. She inspires her own children to live life to the fullest.

"Living in the U.S., I see much stress and so many people working very hard to make a lot of money. In my country, money and things are not as important as being close to friends and family and not as important as trying different ways of living. In Nicaragua, I saw people hating others because they were poor or had different ideas—this led to a revolution between the Sandinistas and the Somozan government that almost destroyed the country. There is so much poverty in Nicaragua because there is no way for the poor to go to school. In my own family, my father could only afford to send my brothers to college. This was the greatest disappointment for me. It meant I had to give up on my dream of becoming a teacher. My father believed it was more important for men to have an education and that women should stay home and raise children.

I know that with an education, we can become successful, have more opportunities and improve ourselves. If I had a chance to go to college today, I'd study painting. Because I didn't go to school, I'm constantly trying to learn and experience new things. I love painting, discovering new ways of dressing, dancing and eating. I also love meeting different kinds of people. I know that nobody's perfect, and this helps me accept others as they are. Being open makes it easier to be happy."

Nubia Leonor Filice, 57
Homemaker & Former Administrative Assistant
Palo Cedro, California, United States
(Originally from Managua, Nicaragua)

"As a person who overanalyzes the meaning and purpose of life to the point where I can no longer enjoy it, my mom grounds me with optimism and encouragement. She always tells me that happiness is a choice, a way of being and living—and that happiness is there for me if I could only realize it upon myself. My mom has a natural ability to forgive and to love unconditionally. I see

it in one of her favorite pastimes—taking care of plants and flowers. The care and love she gives to her plants is a representation of the unconditional love she gives to people. My mom taught me to embrace change, to live one day at a time, to simply choose to be happy and enjoy and appreciate every waking moment. She inspires me to retain some balance and peace of mind in life."

Albert Filice, 29
Teacher
Scottsdale, Arizona, United States
(Originally from Palo Cedro, California)

32

Always do your best.

Make the most of every opportunity life presents to you.

Justice Akuchie is an engineer with empathy. Growing up as a member of a middle-class family in a country with a lot of poverty, Justice feels obligated to always do his best.

"I try to do my best in all situations and fully utilize any opportunity life affords me, because there are hundreds of millions of less fortunate people that would give anything to be in my position. It is unfair and disrespectful to them to squander those opportunities.

Looking back, there wasn't a single event that shaped my philosophy of life. I believe it was the compound effect of growing up in a third-world country and always being surrounded by people in poverty. I'm from a middle-class family, and my parents always tried to help others who were less fortunate. I knew these people personally and quickly understood that, for the most part, they would never have an opportunity to improve their situation. Poverty was forced onto them. Because of what I have observed my entire life, I am blessed with humility. I have no ego, and I am grateful for my lot in life."

Justice Akuchie, 24
Chemical Engineer
Houston, Texas, United States
(Originally from Port-Harcourt, Rivers, Nigeria)

Practicing What You Preach

Staying in touch with your roots and living your ideologies

33 Always stay true to yourself.
No one knows what is best for you, better than you do.

Photo by Leah Gordon

Pratibha Parmar was born in Nairobi, Kenya and migrated to the U.K. when she was eleven years old. She has been an activist for her entire life—striving to make the world a better place for women and people of color. She collaborated with author Alice Walker to create *Warrior Marks*, a documentary-film educating the world about female genital mutilation, and worked on a host of other equity-promoting projects and films. In 2000 she embarked on her most personal project of all—she wrote and directed her first feature length narrative film *Nina's Heavenly Delights*. The semi-autobiographical film reveals her story of falling in love with a Pakistani woman in the U.K. Pratibha believes the greatest accomplishment one can have is to be true to oneself.

"Over the years, I've learned that it is not in my DNA to be anyone other than who I am. The only way to do that is to be true and honest with myself. In my film, *Nina's Heavenly Delights,* I wanted to celebrate the joy of embracing one's true self and in this case it happens to be an Indian girl who falls in love with another woman. My film shows different ways of living and loving, and that true happiness is found in being true to yourself.'"

Pratibha Parmar, 48
Film Director
London, United Kingdom
(Originally from Nairobi, Kenya)

Ranjana Sah was a typical kid in the village of Janakpur, Nepal. She was a silly, healthy, happy-go-lucky little girl that loved to play and always had a can-do attitude. But there was something that separated her from the other girls in her village—Ranjana had only one breast.

Although Ranjana confronted a lot of social stigma as a result, she believes that her birth defect ultimately helped her learn to be true to herself at a young age.

"I was born with only one breast. My birth father started trying to arrange my marriage when I was only nine or ten. He thought if I got married young enough, we could hide the fact that I only had one breast. I was still

Photo by Collin Krauthamer

a kid. I knew I wasn't ready to get married. When my dad would bring the families of potential husbands over to the house to meet me, I would misbehave. I would hide. I would shout and tell them I wasn't ready to get married. Eventually, my dad gave up. As I grew up and my body started to develop, people treated me differently. Girls would make fun of me.

When I was twelve, the best thing in my life happened. My aunt's family in Davis, California, adopted me. Of course it was a little hard at first, because I didn't speak much English. But I made a lot of Mexican friends who helped me along, and nobody really gave me a hard time. I was still shy and embarrassed about my body though. I used to change in the bathroom instead of the locker room for gym class. My adopted mom sometimes helped me stuff half of my bra, but that didn't feel right. When I was sixteen, my gym teacher asked me why I was afraid to be around the other girls. I told her and she talked to my adopted parents about constructive surgery. My adopted parents paid for that surgery and gave me a breast. That was the most life-changing experience I ever had. It defines my identity as a woman.

When I was ready to get married, my adopted mom and dad went back to Nepal to help arrange my marriage. After they found a match, I went and met my prospective husband and told him all about myself—I even told him about the fact that I had only one real breast. He said he didn't mind and that he would love me just the way I was. My husband made alot of sacrifices and struggled alot after arriving here because of the language barrier; but together, we are making it and doing our best to raise our two children. I really don't know what would have happened to me if I were still in Nepal. I might not be alive. I don't think a husband would have known how to accept me with just one breast. I wouldn't have had a normal marriage or sex life. Here, I feel like I can be myself. I wanted to be a nurse, but I couldn't because of language. Now, my dream is to help my family achieve what I couldn't achieve. I want my kids to be something—I want them to see the possibilities."

Ranjana Sah, 32
Daycare Provider
Davis, California, United States
(Originally from Janakpur, Nepal)

Before complaining, take action.

There is always at least one variable in every situation within your control.

Mika Fujita quit her corporate job in hopes of finding something that she was more passionate about. During her time off, she learned about the struggles of Japan's newest population and decided to do something—she became a volunteer language teacher for Noshiro's immigrants. The three women pictured here are among those humbly reaping the benefits of Mika's generosity so they can have a better life in Japan.

"I started to see inconsistencies with the way people were treated and became aware of some of the struggles bicultural, bilingual and immigrant families were dealing with. As I learned more, I realized these problems weren't unique to Akita, but that they existed throughout Japan. I knew that if someone didn't do something, things would never change. I went back to graduate school and studied social pedagogy and learned about the problems non-native speakers of English faced in the United States. This helped me understand the issues non-native Japanese speakers in Japan were facing. Rather than talking about what other people should or shouldn't be doing, we should look at our own role first. We should ask ourselves what we, as individuals, can do to make things better."

Mika Fujita, 32
Volunteer Language Teacher
Noshiro, Japan

Read and internalize Don Miguel Ruiz's *The Four Agreements*.

It's the one life-philosophy book that should be mandatory reading for everyone on the planet. If everyone would practice Ruiz's four agreements— to be impeccable with words, to never make assumptions, to never take things personally and to always do our best—the world would be a better place.

"My parents left El Salvador during the civil war in 1980. At the time, they didn't speak much English. When I began school, I didn't speak English. I still remember my first elementary-school teacher, a nun from the Philippines. She was always very frustrated with me and would yell at me. I didn't know what was going on, but I always thought something was wrong with me. Today, I still feel anxious and uneasy about academics.

When I went to college with the High Potential program, my professor assigned us to read *The Four Agreements*. When I read the book, I realized all I could do was my best. I knew I should do everything passionately, acknowledge what I did well, accept things that didn't go well as learning experiences and grow. I started to live the philosophies.

The philosophy about being impeccable with words reminds me to think before I speak and to be in synch with my values as a Catholic Latina. I've learned to open my eyes, and to accept negative experiences of the past as the past. I'm learning that I'm free to express who I am. I want to live a life of integrity and inspire others to discover themselves. "

Ana Canjura, 21
ESL Teacher in Japan
San Francisco, California, United States
(Originally from El Salvador)

Define success not by how much money you have, but by the way you live your life.
Quality relationships and experiences are priceless.

Suman Raj-Grewal was born in Lautoka, Fiji, to a family of nine. Suman's father worked from five a.m. till dark, while her mom took care of the children. Because Suman's family didn't have a lot of money to spare, Suman learned to find happiness in the simplest things in life—playing with her siblings and taking occasional trips to the market to admire all of the pretty bangles and dancing.

"Growing up with no television, no heated running water, no flushable toilets, no dolls, no meat, and watching my parents buy groceries on credit made me very humble. When my family migrated to the United States, it was difficult to figure out where I belonged. My classmates had their own rooms, wore nice clothes and shoes and spoke perfect English, while my whole family lived in a two-bedroom house. I know that it is those difficulties that made me who I am today. Now, my priority in life is raising two decent human beings and setting an example for them. I am grateful for the lessons and the stories I can share with my children. I try to instill the important things in life that cannot be measured by monetary value. I teach them to be loving and understanding, to be conscious and aware of their environment and those around them, to have respect and appreciation for everything in their lives and to pursue their dreams. I take a few minutes a day to ground myself.

It has taken me many years and many life experiences to come to a point where I can express who I am, what my beliefs are, and to be able to say, 'This is Suman.' I am a mom, a wife, a daughter, a daughter-in-law, an aunt, a sister, a friend, a homemaker, a breadwinner and a dancer. I start my day with positive affirmations and end my day by journaling or quietly reflecting. At the end of the day, I just hope I am making a difference."

Suman Raj-Grewal, 41
Bank Manager
Hercules, California, United States
(Originally from Lautoka, Fiji)

Strive to understand issues from multiple perspectives.

There are at least two sides to every story.

More than 60,000 Sri Lankans have been killed, and more than 240 suicide bombings have been carried out as the result of the ethnic conflict between Singhalese and Tamils that began in 1956. Checkpoints are prevalent throughout the entire country. Reita Ganayagam, a Tamil, and Kesara Premachandra, a Singhalese, have been affected by Sri Lanka's ethnic conflict in vastly different ways, but have a common vision for peace.

I knew how much Tamils were suffering, and I knew that we needed freedom, so I joined the Libertarian Tamil Tigers of Elam [LTTE]. There is nothing that says that I cannot have children, but young Tamil people are suffering so much, I would rather serve my country than bring children into the world. Tamil people are living in fear. There are checkpoints everywhere, armed military men on the streets and in schools. We feel like slaves in our own country. We want Tamils and Singhalese to live together peacefully even though our cultures are different. If we can accomplish peace and normalcy, children will grow up that way. If not, the children will be left to continue the fight."

"I was displaced from Jaffna in 1995. Wherever my family went, there was chaos, shellings and bombings. I watched people die in front of me. My brother died. My father was a driver and now he's a gardener. My whole family was displaced. We don't have a house anymore, because it was destroyed by the army.

Reita Ganayagam, 27
*Member, Women's Division of the
Libertarian Tamil Tigers of Elam*
Mannar, Sri Lanka

"I see stories in the Tamil newspapers detailing tirades of Singhalese soldiers in Tamil villages, and then I hear about rebel Tigers killing innocent civilians in an effort to send a message. I remember it all—the Pettah train-station bombing, where nearly 1,000 people were killed during rush hour, and the Central Bank bombing, where 2,000 people were killed by the initial blast and hundreds more died of suffocation after getting trapped underground. My mother was working in Colombo at the time. I used to be on edge waiting for her to come home. I have lost neighbors, friends and family, both Singhalese and Tamil, as a result of this war. I see that the LTTE is trying to fight for the little piece of land they call home, but I can't support its tactics.

I escaped the war in Sri Lanka to enter a different war. I'm in the U.S., a country that is constantly involved with war. War has created a cycle of hatred. New generations are born into wars and forced to pick sides. I really believe the only solution to the problems both within my country and the world at large is education. Learning Tamil has enabled me to gain a better understanding of the situation in my country. I think Singhalese should learn about the culture and language of Tamils, and Tamils should learn about the culture and language of Singhalese.

I feel blessed to have Singhalese and Tamils coming together in my own family. My uncle married a Tamil woman. When his daughter, my cousin, got married, she incorporated Singhalese, Tamil, Catholic and Jewish rituals into her ceremony to represent both her culture and her husband's culture. It was a beautiful marriage of culture, religion and language. It was a ritual that might have never happened at home. If Tamils and Singhalese could embrace each other the way my family has, I think we would all be able to blend in our cultural values and come together as one."

Kesara Premachandra, 21
Singhalese-American College Student
Northridge, California, United States
(Originally from Kandy, Sri Lanka)

38

Meditate.
Take time out of each day to live in the moment and count your blessings.

The children of Calcutta, India's servants, rickshaw drivers and homeless families gather at Navjyoti School with a volunteer staff to study so they can break the cycle of illiteracy and poverty. They may not have much, but they start each day meditating and counting their blessings.

Doctoral student Sarah Reed has never made it to India. Yet she has found peace of mind in putting the Eastern practices of yoga and meditation into action.

"When I was in seventh grade, my friends and I loved the Beatles and wanted to be hippies. We knew that the Beatles were into Ravi Shankar and meditation, so we tried to do the same thing. We used to pretend to meditate because we didn't think we knew how.

When I got to college, I learned the true value of meditation. I started practicing yoga and have kept up ever since. It helps me keep everything in balance. I study science, which is male-centered and based in the Western way of thinking. The Eastern tradition of yoga balances that out. Now, I truly love to meditate and do it almost every day. It helps me cope with the extreme business of going about life from eight a.m. to midnight every day. It helps me ground myself. I use yoga scripts to help overcome self-esteem issues and set aside the nervousness and self-doubt that come along with the pressure of doing presentations. It helps me keep life in perspective."

Sarah Reed, 29
Environmental Science Doctoral Student
Virginia, Minnesota, United States

39

Travel to learn about yourself and the world, not to escape.

No matter how far you go, you can never get away from yourself. Instead, embrace the opportunity and get to know yourself better.

Carrie Kroon was adopted from Korea when she was three. She returned to her homeland for the first time as a high-school student. That trip changed Carrie's life.

"I always knew I was adopted because my parents and brothers were white, and I didn't look like them. My parents never hid it, but we never talked about it. I was always just Carrie. When my parents first adopted me, people criticized them. Some kids at school were mean to me. They'd make fun of my eyes, tell me I was different and make me feel like an outcast. I used to cry every day in elementary school.

When I was in high school, I got the chance to visit Korea. This experience changed my life. Going back to Korea was a chance for me to learn about my roots. Looking back, I realize that before I went there, part of my identity was missing. I knew I was Korean, but I didn't know anything about Korea or the culture. When I arrived in Seoul, I remember looking around and noticing that everyone looked like me. It was my first time being in the majority. I was used to being surrounded by whites. I also realized that although I was Korean, I was different from the Koreans around me. I was Americanized and everyone knew that. The trip made me a stronger person. I became proud of my background. After I came back, the comments people made didn't bother me as much, because I was more secure with myself. I knew who I was and where I came from. I also knew that someday I'd want to return and find my biological family.

Everyone should have the experience of traveling. Sometimes, people in the U.S. get tricked into thinking that the way of the U.S. is the only way or the best way, but there are so many different ways of life. If people go and experience the world, they will see just how many ways there are, and their lives will become richer."

Carrie Kroon, 27
Office Manager
Oakland, California, United States
(Originally from Seoul, Korea)

Hortencia Ruiz was fully able to embrace her cultural roots for the first time when she traveled to Mexico.

"People don't assume I'm Mexican. Mexicans don't see me as Mexican, but I know that I am. I always went to a Catholic, mostly white school. I used to feel embarrassed about being different. My dad was a landscaper; he used to pick me up in his work truck. My dad didn't know any English. He came to the U.S. when he was sixteen with one brother. He thought we would have more opportunities here, and hoped to someday make a better life for his family.

I visited Mexico when I was sixteen with my brother and cousin. Having to speak Spanish non-stop for three weeks with relatives helped me reconnect with my Mexican roots and learn how great it is to be a part of a Mexican family."

Hortencia Ruiz, 22
College Student
Sacramento, California, United States

Treasure your friends.

They are irreplaceable.

As a motivational speaker, Veraunda Jackson inspires young men and women to take charge of their lives, treat each other well and be courageous. In the spirit of being consistent and practicing what she preaches, Veraunda has learned to never take friends for granted.

"Over the years, I have watched my relationships with friends change. I have lost friends and made new ones. I believe the greatest asset in a relationship is finding the value of the other person. Everyone brings something different to the table. I ask myself if I can meet this person where they are, and if I can love and appreciate them for who they are. I have also come to realize that the saying, 'People are in your life for a reason, a season or a lifetime,' is definitely true. It makes me value the time I share with friends. Whether they are in my life for a season or a reason, I accept that and cherish the time we spend together."

Veraunda Jackson, 37
Author, Attorney & Motivational Speaker
Orlando, Florida, United States

Act on your dreams.

Most dreams don't come true without effort.

Christian Herrera aspired to be a professional soccer player. Although he wasn't able to realize his dream, he came up with an alternative plan in later life.

"I've learned that when we have a dream, we have to work on it for it to become real, otherwise the years will pass us by. When I was younger I dreamt of becoming a soccer player. When I was seventeen years old, I left the Dominican Republic to try and make my dream a reality. I attended a year of high school in a small town in Wisconsin to learn English. My goal was to find an American university with a soccer program and try to get drafted. I wanted that more than anything, but it didn't work out. When I turned twenty, I let my dream go. I did everything that was expected of me. I graduated from the local college, got a business job, got married and had a beautiful son. I have a great life now and a beautiful family, but I still wonder what might have happened if I would have worked harder, if I hadn't given up so easily.

Knowing that I can not turn back time, I wanted to find something else I was passionate about. One day, I found an advertisement for a sports management master's program at a university in Spain. After a lot of thinking, I knew that I had to go, even if it meant leaving my son and wife behind for a year. If I didn't go and try to pursue something that I was passionate about now, I might never do it. I don't know what will happen after this, because there are no guarantees. I have spent a lot of my savings and taken a lot of risks. But at the same time, I am proud of what I am doing. I know that I am working towards something that I want, and I know that following dreams takes sacrifices."

Christian Herrera, 30
Graduate Student
Barcelona, Spain
(Originally from Santo Domingo, Dominican Republic)

Make yourself happy first.

You can't please everyone, and you can lose yourself trying.

Praveena Kumar witnessed alcoholism and abuse in her home throughout her childhood. Praveena's mother put everyone else's needs before her own. Watching her mother struggle inspired Praveena to live life for herself.

"I had an alcoholic father who was physically and verbally abusive towards my mom. My mom stayed for the sake of my three brothers and me. It would have been hard for her to leave even if she wanted to, because she had only an elementary-school education. In 1993, my dad left and I think that's the best thing he ever did. When my brothers and I reflect on all the things we've gone through, we are amazed that we have turned out so well. Our experiences impacted many of our life decisions. I don't drink at all, and my brothers drink very moderately because we have seen what alcohol can do.

I am happy with my life now. I follow the general guidelines of society, but I don't make decisions for the sake of pleasing others. I have a mind of my own and I have to follow my instincts. I have been dating the same man for about ten years. We were engaged for a period of time, but decided not to get married. I saw so many marriages falling apart, and I knew what had happened in my own family. I think a lot of people get married because it's what society expects them to do. My boyfriend and I are still together. He is my best friend. You don't have to be engaged to be in a relationship. You can be in a relationship just because you want to. You don't have to define it through marriage. Marriage is like every issue in life. You have to do what is right for you. Otherwise, you'll just be going through the motions."

Praveena Kumar, 39
Clinical Dietician
Suva, Fiji

Communicate openly and honestly.

The world would be a better place if we all said what we meant and meant what we said.

Learning to communicate openly and honestly strengthened the quality of Christine Garvin's life.

"I think the main source of all conflict is a lack of open and honest communication. Throughout life, I've gone through ups and downs without ever dealing with the real issues that were affecting me. When something went wrong, I had a pattern of getting angry, not caring and then feeling angry again. I used to let everything build up until I became physically ill.

A few years ago, I began a graduate program in holistic health. I learned that in order to be whole, we have to deal with all aspects of ourselves. We can't do that without openly communicating. Open communication allows us to take care of our needs in a way that is not angry or confrontational. I recently went through a disempowering situation with a friend. Rather than repressing my feelings, I wrote an e-mail that shared my perspective and point of view. When I sent the e-mail, I literally felt my body let go. It affirmed that mind, body and spirit really are connected. Learning to communicate openly and honestly has changed my life.

If we all communicated openly and honestly in a way that wasn't hurtful to others, there would be fewer wars between other countries, fewer wars on the streets and fewer wars at work. The world would be a better place."

Christine Garvin, 28
Nutritionist
Rocky Mount, North Carolina, United States

Put karma into practice.

If you treat others well and release positive energy into the world, you will be rewarded. If you act selfishly, you may attract negative energy.

DJ Cheb I Sabbah has been sharing music with the world for decades. He has produced several albums with Six-Degrees, and plays his music everywhere from San Francisco's Haight Street, to Los Angeles, to Spain, to Paris and, of course, India. He sees music as a universal means for connecting all types of people. Cheb I Sabbah believes people have an obligation to promote peace and tolerance and eliminate poverty. He makes a conscious effort to put karma into practice through his music and in the way he lives his life.

"Do what you can to promote tolerance, and solve poverty and ignorance. Use whatever means you can to do something positive. If you earn $100, give $10 to charity. If you can create music or dance to it, do it. Music makes people feel good and creates positive vibrational energy. The world is based on vibrational energy. We should all take part and distribute positivity whenever we have a chance.

Respect everything and everyone. All humans are searching for something and have some kind of aspiration. Everyone's looking for love. Even a murderer or the worst criminal in the world wants to be loved. Showing love is the basic way to make someone happy. If you make one or more persons happy by helping them eat, see or generate love, they will send you positive vibrational energy, and your positive deeds will multiply by the millions."

Cheb I Sabbah, 60
Musician
San Francisco, California, United States
(Originally from Algeria)

Onee Bhaumik teaches at Navjyoti School in Calcutta, India in hopes of 'undoing' the cycles of poverty and illiteracy that have plagued many throughout India and West Bengal. Working with the poorest members of society has helped Onee develop a greater appreciation for life.

"If you want the world to be a little more beautiful, you should do something for someone to give them a little happiness and feel happy yourself."

Onee Bhaumik, 56
Teacher, Navjyoti School
Calcutta, India

45

Believe in yourself.
If you don't believe in yourself, who will?

In the United States, one in four women experience sexual assault in their lifetime. Shaleen Kumar is among the women in that statistic. It wasn't until Shaleen started to believe in herself that she was able to heal.

"In college, I went to a dorm party and someone spiked my drink. I ended up getting raped that night. It was my choice to drink, so I blamed myself for a long time. I felt like it was all my fault. I was extremely depressed and even attempted suicide. I fell behind in school. I didn't tell anyone what happened to me for five years.

One day, I saw a video at school that inspired me to reach out. I decided to tell my aunt what happened to me. That is when the healing process began. I started to have positive thoughts about myself after that. Even though I couldn't undo the rape, I could focus on graduating. It took me two extra years to finish college, but I believed in myself and I successfully received a bachelor's degree in psychology. What I went through makes me want to help others. Someday, I hope to set up an organization to help people who have experienced trauma. The best advice I can offer others who might be affected by sexual assault is to believe in yourself and tell someone what happened. It is the only way to heal."

Shaleen Kumar, 26
Caseworker for Autistic Children
Berkeley, California, United States

Overcoming

Obstacles &

Stereotypes

Being the best that you can be

Challenge racism, sexism and all forms of oppression whenever you have a chance.

Confront ignorance and hate with love and unity.

On a warm autumn Saturday afternoon in 2001, twenty members of the Ku Klux Klan gathered on the steps of the state capitol in St. Paul, Minnesota, to exercise their First Amendment rights. More than 1,500 protestors showed up to greet the KKK that day. Each time a member of the KKK shouted a message of hate, the protesters drowned out the sound. They used pots and pans as percussion instruments, shouted "no room for hate," danced, sang and used all of their positive energy to reject the white supremacist messages and promote peace. Minnesota Senator Paul Wellstone, who dedicated his life to the fight for social justice, stopped by that afternoon to join the counter-protesters in his blue button-down shirt, carrying a bullhorn. (That was one of Paul Wellstone's last fights for social justice, as less than one year later, he died in a plane crash.) What could have been a day of hatred and disaster turned into a day of unity, love and peace. Every voice makes a difference.

In 2003, the V-Day: Until the Violence Ends movement and *The Vagina Monologues* became a tradition at Saint Mary's College of California. Playwright Eve Ensler's mission is to end the silence and break the cycle of violence affecting women throughout the world. Each year the students performing the controversial play are met with resistance from individuals who feel the play is "un-Catholic'" and unnecessary. However, the women participating in *The Vagina Monologues* have found it to be a truly transformational process. They are honored to contribute to the cause of ending violence against women.

Photo by Collin Krauthamer

Shana Dhillon was sexually assaulted by the man she most admired when she was fourteen years old. Participating in V-Day helped Shana connect with other women and heal.

"Being a survivor of rape, I always felt that I had to hide my experience because of what others might think, and also to preserve my reputation. By keeping quiet about my experience, I was falling into the cycle and keeping people unaware of how prevalent rape is in our very own community. *The Vagina Monologues* gave me a voice to inform people about what goes on behind closed doors. I gained the courage not to care about what people may think of me and learned that it was not my fault.

I feel as if I'm a completely different person after taking part in *The Vagina Monologues*. I feel so much stronger, much more confident and astonishingly positive about life in general. It helped me heal because I feel as if I was finally able to put my past behind me and work towards a better future in helping other women and girls that have been through what I have, or worse."

Shana Dhillon, 20
College Student
Fremont, California, United States

Liz Johnson understands the complexity of violence against women. Liz is a feminist, an ally to marginalized populations and the daughter of a registered sex offender. Staying true to the cause while continuing to love her father has made Liz a stronger woman, determined to break the cycles of violence and abuse. V-Day has helped Liz make sense of life.

"(Participating in) *The Vagina Monologues* has helped me heal by standing up against the marginalization of women. My father is a registered sex offender, and that has caused a lot of pain in my life. When it comes to sexual assault, people often forget about the other victims in the situation, and the families of the perpetrators themselves. As a child, I was often marginalized because of my father's situation, which made me feel ashamed of my family and who I was. The V-Day movement helped me see that I wasn't the only one that was affected by gender violence and helped me learn to love myself. I learned from my fellow cast members to be open to new ideas. It is great to see how through the process of preparing for V-Day and reflecting on our own life experiences, we are able to heal (and connect with each other)."

Liz Johnson, 22
College Student
Ukiah, California, United States

Challenge yourself to overcome stereotypes.

By virtue of being human beings with a set of life experiences, we all hold some stereotypes. Be willing to reconsider your perspectives and challenge yourself.

A little girl is pictured shopping in Asaka, Tokyo; while a family in Akita enjoys a traditional meal at home. These are two example of the different cultures in Japan. Mika Fujita believes that Japan will be a stronger country when its residents realize how diverse a ninety-nine percent homogeneous country can be.

"We have to reframe our way of thinking about culture. People don't realize how multicultural Japan is. People of different ages, from different regions of Japan, from different families, with different experiences, have different ways of life and different ideas. Without realizing how broad the term 'culture' can be, it's easy to group everyone together, and assume everyone from the same country is the same. We can't say 'nani jin da kara' (she is like x because she is of a certain nationality); instead, we have to look at people on a case-by-case basis."

Mika Fujita, 32
Linguist
Noshiro, Japan

89

See every struggle as a blessing in disguise.
Struggles give us the strength to persevere.

Buck Singh Dhesi was born in Kenya and raised in the neighboring country of Uganda. When Buck turned thirty-eight, he was forced to leave his homeland after Idi Amin asked all foreigners to vacate the country within ninety days. Buck went to Canada as a refugee and started over.

"On September 27, 1972, I entered Calgary, Canada as a refugee. In Africa I had been a successful engineer, but in Canada, I had to start from scratch. I arrived with no money in my pocket and without shoes on my feet, as they had been taken from me at the airport. I had to realize that I wasn't going through this alone—156,000 families were going through the same thing. I realized that material things really didn't matter and that the most valuable things were health and life itself. When you're on the ground and you can't go any further down, there really is nowhere to go but up. It's up to you to do your best to stay upbeat and positive.

I worked as a linesman for five years in Canada. I later came to California to work for a car dealership for fifteen years, and now have a 160-acre almond farm in the Central Valley. I love California, but Africa will always be my motherland. Even if my relatives weren't there, I'd continue to go back. I love the land and the people. I love being able to greet people in their own language. It's sad to see how much people have to struggle to get by. It is a myth that Africa is a dark country to be avoided. Given the opportunity and access to an education, everyone will do well regardless of what their race is."

Buck Singh Dhesi, 72
Almond Farmer
Bakersfield, California, United States
(Originally from Kampala, Uganda)

Be resilient.

A strong core can get you through life's most challenging predicaments and tragedies.

Joyce Aballo has witnessed more violence and hardship at the young age of twenty than most people experience in a lifetime. Resiliency is what keeps her going.

"I came from the north two years ago because of the rebels. The rebels killed my father, took my brothers and killed one of them. They burned our house down. My mom disappeared a few years ago and I don't know what happened to her. I feel bad sometimes.

I came to Kampala to start a new life and take care of my brothers. I got a job in a shop where I earn 50,000 shillings ($25 per month). I never got to go to school. After my father died, I needed to help with digging and gardening, and there was no time for me to study. I want my brothers to finish school so they can have chances I didn't have.

Someday I will find someone to love me and share my life with. For now, I'm happy that I have an auntie close by, and that I can take care of my brothers."

Joyce Abalo, 20
Shopkeeper
Kampala, Uganda

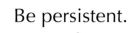

Be persistent.

No matter how many times you fall, get back up and try again. Some of us are born with more economic resources and access than others. After that, what separates those of us who accomplish our dreams from those who give up is the amount of persistence and resiliency we have.

Sulinda Khoe left Indonesia to go to college at St. Cloud State University in Minnesota. After graduating, Sulinda landed a job at a bank in

Los Angeles and had the option of staying. She remembers having a good life in the United States, but wanting more.

"I studied in the U.S. and found a job at a bank in Los Angeles, but I wanted more. I had always dreamed of having a business and wanted to be closer to my family, so I went back to Indonesia.

When I got home, things didn't work as planned. I tried many things and struggled to make progress or to understand my purpose. But I hung in there. Now, I have been given an opportunity to try opening a handbag shop. It's different than what I envisioned, and I know it will be challenging, but it makes me feel like my long struggle is finally paying off. I am finally going to have my own business."

Sulinda Khoe, 29
Entrepreneur
Jakarta, Indonesia

Being in New York on 9/11 and watching the Twin Towers crumble helped Genevieve Castellino realize that life was too short not to pursue her dreams.

"What I've internalized is: never look back. You'll always find things that went wrong. Rather than dwelling, keep going and do better next time. People talk about luck, but it's not about luck. It's about persisting in something. You don't magically find yourself in the right place at the right time. Chances are you have taken steps to put yourself in the 'right place' at the 'right time.'

I came to the U.S. in 1989 during the recession, got a degree in filmmaking and later found a well-paying, corporate IT job. After watching the World Trade Center collapse on 9/11, I couldn't help but reassess and re-envision my life. I thought about what I would have to say for my life if I had been in a building that had collapsed. I could have said that I had a very comfortable life, but that would have been it. I decided I would take a huge risk. I had always been passionate about having a voice, finding an outlet for voice and film. I decided to take a year off of my job to produce a film. I created the film *Quarter Life Crisis*, exploring the complicated concept of love in the South Asian community.

Producing this film has helped me develop really thick skin. I've learned that the only way to ever be successful is to be comfortable being rejected

over and over and to keep finding ways to get back up again. It is easy for people to get paralyzed by everything that did not happen or did not go right in life. The best thing to do is to get over yourself and try to see what your contribution might have been. When something goes wrong, step back, assess, zone in on one or two things that you could have done differently. You can rectify the situation, and more doors will open."

Genevieve Castellino, 40
Film Producer
Metuchen, New Jersey, United States
(Originally from Mumbai, India)

93

51 Don't judge people whose perspective is vastly different from yours.

Nobody has had the opportunity to explore the world and the issues of life in the same way you have.

When Ivan Dominguez was eight, his family closed up their small store in Juarez, Mexico, and headed to the U.S. in hopes of starting a new life. As the one English speaker in his family, Ivan was forced to grow up fast. He has had to encounter a fair share of stereotypes, but he refuses to see himself as a victim and is doing everything he can to empower the next generation in his job at an after-school teen center.

"Sometimes, people think of immigrants as job stealers, criminals and welfare seekers. It's part of human nature; when people don't know something, they'll say it's bad or good, because they don't know.

When a Mexican family comes over the border, chances are they are not going to take someone else's job away. The parents are most likely going to have jobs in restaurants washing dishes, in factories doing manual labor or in fields doing agricultural work. If the children are able to study and get a good education, they may have opportunities that their parents did not. However, first there are many obstacles for the children to overcome. At the same time as children are encouraged to stay off drugs and stay out of gangs, some grow up in neighborhoods that are bombarded with those things. They're looking for a place to fit in and something to be a part of.

I love having a job that allows me to be here for teens who are struggling with these issues. There were some kids that I couldn't do much for. Many kids confront drugs, gangs and peer pressure. The hardest part is that sometimes there are kids who don't want to be associated with a gang, but dress a certain way and take consequences for it. It's hard to see kids struggling. I'll get my reward when I see the kids go away, do something for themselves and come back and tell me that I helped them in some way, and now they have a job and are the father or mother of two kids."

Ivan Dominguez, 21
Youth Counselor & Musician
El Paso, Texas, United States
(Originally from Juarez, Mexico)

Be open-minded.

Having an open mind allows you to consider and learn from multiple perspectives.

Pursuing his dream while respecting his parents' values has helped Kim Dao learn the value of open-mindedness.

"Being from a traditional Vietnamese family, I grew up feeling there were only certain labels I could wear. I wanted to go to art school, but my family frowned upon that. I ended up going to business school as a compromise. Even though that wasn't my first choice, I know I'm privileged because my parents never had the chance to attend college. I have found ways to squeeze creativity into the field of business. As one of the few Asian gay males at a Catholic college, I face another set of challenges finding my place.

I try to be diverse and open-minded. When you're a twenty-something, you kind of know what's right and what's wrong, but still make mistakes sometimes. Some people have a clear notion of which perspective is right and which is wrong, but I think you have to stand in the middle and be objective about things sometimes. It doesn't matter where you stand, it matters who you stand with. I'm not out to fight, but to promote understanding. The only way to understand is to get together and speak. If you don't get an educated view, you make assumptions and that doesn't do anyone any good. Don't be afraid of difference; be afraid of the same. Difference drives change. When you surround yourself with only people who are the same as you, you lose the chance to learn."

Kim Dao, 21
Artist
San Jose, California, United States
(Originally from Mo Tho, Vietnam)

95

Don't assume that everything you hear is true.

The old saying, "To assume is to make an a** out of (yo)u and me," is often true.

Calcutta's Park Street is like San Francisco's Market Street or New York City's Central Park, a place where people of different classes are forced to interact. The many poor children who are not in school spend their days shining shoes, selling gum or trying to befriend tourists and wealthy locals in hopes of receiving some spare rupees.

Park Street is not an anomaly. With as many as 120 million Indian children out of school and as many as sixty million children in jobs mixing chemicals, weaving carpets or assembling products, and helping their parents, India has one of the world's most inaccessible education systems and one of the youngest work forces.

These are the faces of children who have slipped through the cracks, who are caught in the cycle of poverty and illiteracy. They may ask you for some rupees when you pass them on the street—not because they are lazy, but because they are hungry.

Many of us are guilty of making assumptions about issues ranging from homelessness to the situation in other countries. We decide, based on what we've seen in the news, that the people in a particular place are a certain way or assume that people on the streets must be at fault for their situation. However, I've found these assumptions to be largely inaccurate.

Inspired by Sanjay, 6 and Pria, 9
Homeless Children
Calcutta, India

North Americans and Cubans have been socialized to be skeptical of one another. The young Cuban and American men and women pictured here had a chance to rethink their assumptions in Havana, Cuba.

"North Americans must know that we think they are persons, just as we are. We know that the government's policies have nothing to do with the people."

Yasser Rodriguez, 24
English Teacher
Havana, Cuba

Bloom where you are planted.

Vow to make the best of your life, no matter what geographical location you are in.

Anne Nelson spent the first thirty-one years of her life in Scotland. She met her American husband when he was stationed in her hometown. After getting married, Anne left her country for the first time—first moving to California to start a family and later moving to her husband's hometown in Whitehall, Wisconsin.

"In 2000, my husband became ill and died. I found myself alone with my two boys in the town where my husband's roots were. I thought about moving back to Scotland, but realized this had become my new home. I had connected to the people here, gotten involved in the community and made friends. I wasn't ready to leave and start over again. I worked in the City Café for a while, then at a lawyer's office and at the City Hall. Then I got an eye infection and my eyesight went bad, so I had to quit working. Scottish people are survivors and fighters. We know that there were good times in the past, but that we have to live in the present. If you dwell on the past, you'll never get on with it.

Now, I spend all my spare time volunteering. I volunteer at events for the hospital and the nursing home, and for Special Olympics. I chair Ladies Aid and deliver meals to senior citizens. I think that as long as you live in a community, you should help others. I know someday I might be in a nursing home; I'll need help, and hopefully, someone will want to help me. I know not to plan, because you never know what tomorrow's going to bring. We might as well make the best of where we're at today. Life is fun. We should enjoy it and bloom where we are planted."

Anne Nelson, 58
Mother, Friend & Volunteer
Whitehall, Wisconsin, United States
(Originally from Eyr, Scotland)

Appreciate the place you come from, no matter where it is or how it is perceived.

It helped make you the person you are today.

Allan Campbell idealized the thought of leaving Texas for her entire life. After she left, she realized that there really is no place like home.

"If you don't appreciate the place you come from, no matter where it is, rethink it. I grew up in Austin, Texas and was really excited to leave for college. After I left, I really started to appreciate home. My family is there. My closest friends are there. Whenever I go home, I know I can truly be myself and not have to worry about stereotypes. The rest of the world seems to have so many stereotypes about Texas and Texans. I want everyone to know that there are many kinds of Texans. We're not all stupid. We don't all raise cattle. We don't all talk with a thick accent. We can't be easily defined. I'm a Texan and I love to dance, surf and design clothes. I grew up in a free-spirited city and have a racially diverse group of friends."

Allan Campbell, 20
Fashion Design Student
San Francisco, California, United States
(Originally from Austin, Texas)

56 Appreciate difference.
It makes the world more beautiful.

As a transgender person, Apaulo Hart has encountered many people who are uncomfortable with Apaulo's transgender identity. Apaulo's uniqueness inspires Apaulo to learn from as many different kinds of people as possible.

"I identify as a transgender person. I believe that gender is socially constructed. Children are taught that there is a specific way for girls to be and another for boys—girls are given pink things and boys are given blue things. I think gender is fluid. I always knew that I was different and that I didn't clearly fit into any gender. I grew up in a strict Christian home, went to a Christian school and I always felt 'wrong.' I felt like I was messed up or perverted. It wasn't until after I graduated from high school that I started to become comfortable with who I was. I recently decided to begin hormone therapy so I can look the way I want to look. Some people are very critical about hormone therapy because it alters your body. But it's really no different than putting on makeup, coloring your hair or getting piercings—and people do those things every day.

My philosophy on life is that we should talk and get people's thoughts rather than making assumptions. People should talk to as many different kinds of people as possible. There are so many perspectives in the world; what's the point of life if we can't learn from each other?"

Apaulo Hart, 25
Artist & Barista
Oakland, California, United States
(Originally from Phoenix, Arizona)

Lindsey Rosellini learned to appreciate difference when she followed her roots back to Italy.

"I went to Italy with a professor who had a unique approach to life. Her perspective was that difference was inherent and that it shouldn't really be an issue. My experience solidified the notion that everyone is different, and we need to appreciate and embrace that. As long as difference doesn't harm anyone else, why should it ever be a problem? In my own life, I have refrained from 'coming out' to my family out of a fear for how others would respond to my difference. When I am able to share that part of myself with my family, I'll be free in ways that other people are not. I'll be untouchable."

Lindsey Rosellini, 22
Communications Student
Bellingham, Washington,
United States

57 Make friends from all corners of the world.

This will make your world a more interesting place.

"Making friends of all religious, cultural and national backgrounds has made my own world larger. I was excited when I started to meet people from different countries. I learned about many cultures which were different from mine. It is heartening to know there are so many perspectives on life out there. It is true that the differences of culture, religion, race, socioeconomics and feelings of entitlement to resources have caused a great deal of struggle. But at a more basic level, I have to wonder why we, as humans, feel it is okay to discriminate against each other and treat

Nami Inoue has made it her mission in life to make friends with as many different kinds of people as possible. While at home, she constantly befriends international newcomers and visitors. When she's abroad visiting friends, she goes out of her way to experience culture to the fullest extent possible. Nami's positive that if everyone lived life like her, the world might be a more peaceful place. Nami is pictured here with her Singhalese Sri Lankan friend.

fellow humans so poorly. If everyone, including policymakers and world leaders, could wholeheartedly embrace the idea of having friends in countries all over the world, the world would be a better, more peaceful place. We would have a hard time dropping bombs in countries where our friends lived."

Nami Inoue, 29
English Teacher
Yamagata, Japan

Waiting

Understanding the priceless
virtues of patience and compromise

58

Strive to lead a life of balance.

Balance, along with patience, will make you better at what you do and more pleasant to be around.

Eclectic composer and musician Karsh Kale wears many hats. He is a tabla player, a composer, a musician who has crossed multiple genres, a writer and a father. Karsh has released several albums and traveled for much of his adult life. Integrating patience and balance into his life has helped Karsh become a more effective musician.

"Letting something develop and allowing space to correct yourself and say what you have to say in the right way is very important for composing music. I don't sit in a studio in front of a computer and try to force it. Instead, I sit with a guitar and string and decide what feels right. The life of a musician is one of imbalance, and it inevitably affects the other aspects of life. It's about knowing the right things to do and about being the best that you can be. I'm a father as well as a musician. When I'm in Brooklyn, I have to be a dad as well as someone who goes to the studio. Although I travel a lot, Brooklyn is where my daughter is, so that is where home is."

Karsh Kale, 34
Musician
Brooklyn, New York, United States
(Originally from West Bromwitch, United Kingdom)

Take things one day at a time.

This approach makes the obstacles of life most manageable.

Lupe Galbaldon was born on one side of the border, marked by this sign, and today lives on the other side. She struggles to keep herself afloat in the United States, but by approaching life one day at a time, she perseveres.

"I had to grow up fast. When I was in seventh grade, my mom died and I fell behind in school. I dropped out of school in ninth grade. When I was a teenager with nowhere to go, I turned myself in, to foster care. In trying to make ends meet, I became a 'Jane of all trades.' I've done everything from cooking to maintenance to security.

Now, I'm doing my best to raise my daughter, in a three-bedroom house that we share with eleven other people. With some encourage-ment, I got my GED at El Paso Community College, got a job as a maintenance person at Project Vida and a grant that I want to use for truck-driving school. I really don't believe in the American dream. I want my daughter to accomplish something with her life. I want her to be someone. I've learned the best thing I can do is to take things one day at a time."

Lupe Gabaldon, 37
Construction Worker
El Paso, Texas, United States
(Originally from Juarez, Mexico)

Nona Mock Wyman is a one-of-a-kind woman. She was born in Chinatown in San Francisco and dropped off at an orphanage in Palo Alto as a young child. That was the last time she saw her mother. Nona became so attached to her or-phan sisters that when she reached sixteen and had the option of being adopted, she chose to stay in the orphanage. Nona didn't receive a for-mal college education, but has done everything she has set out to do and more. Nona is the au-thor of *Chopstick Childhood* and is working on her second book *Bamboo Women*. Nona is also the proud owner of Ming Quong, a hip store with global merchandise and a seventies feel, in Walnut Creek, California. She takes pride in making the best of each and every day.

"I'm a rooster and a Gemini, and I feel like I'm on top of the world. Every day, I wake up feeling happy about the day because I love what I do. I love writing and I love the customers that come to my shop. When you find something you really love, you can let yourself get so lost in it that you don't mind putting in hours. When I'm in my shop, I get to hear so many interesting stories about people's lives. Sometimes I give advice and feel surprised about what I've said. The people who come to my store are open-minded, artistic, independent and have a mind of their own. They choose to come here rather than Macy's or Nordstroms, which are just down the road. It's a nice feeling.

When I turned fifty, I started writing affirmations and visualizing my goals. This has made my life even better. I'm grateful to be a woman. I'm calling my next book *Bamboo Woman*, because I really believe a good woman is like bamboo—when the wind blows it bends, but it doesn't break."

Nona Mock Wyman, 74
Writer & Shop Owner
Walnut Creek, California, United States

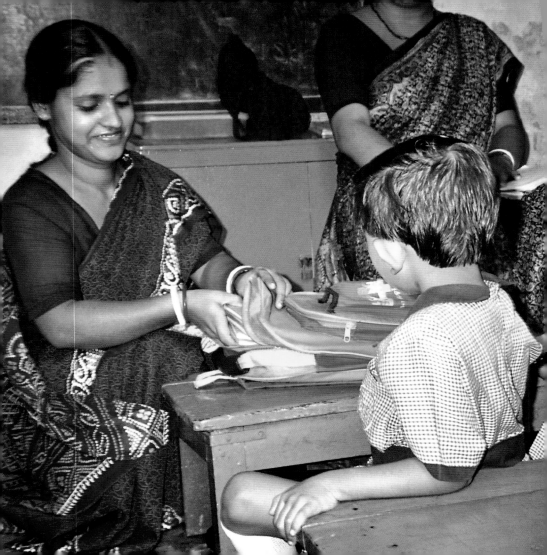

Wait. Patience really is a priceless virtue.

Sow the seeds for change today, see the results tomorrow.

Growing up in the slums along with her four brothers and sisters, Reita Hazra was one of the Calcutta children about to slip through the cracks of the Indian education system, when she discovered the Navjyoti School, just down the road from her home. The school was started by a group of women who wanted to break the cycles of illiteracy and poverty for India's social untouchables. Reita is the daughter of a servant and the wife of a rickshaw driver. She was only able to stay in school until eighth grade. Even so, she is now literate, more educated than her mother and is able to provide a better life for her children than her mother was able to provide for her. She is hoping her own children might get a little further than she did. Reita didn't graduate, but her children will.

"My mom lived next to Navjyoti School and I wanted to educate myself, so I came. I couldn't study long enough to graduate, but I learned so much. Now, I work here as a teacher's assistant and bring my own children to study here. I do this because it's what my heart tells me to do. I have more understanding of the children's backgrounds. It's very nice to be working with them. I hope someday my own children will have the chance to graduate and do something good with their lives."

Reita Hazra, 20
Teacher's Assistant
Calcutta, India

Live in the present.

Make an effort to enjoy every moment of life today, as you never know what tomorrow will bring.

Irma Pena's brother was her best friend in the whole world. While she was watching a baseball game on a sunny afternoon in February 2003, she had an eerie feeling and went home. She learned that her brother had just been in a deadly helicopter crash. Losing her brother inspired Irma to make a conscious effort to live in the present.

"I asked God why he couldn't wait. We were a family of four siblings and my brother was the oldest. My brother was such an angel—he would have given the shirt off his back. Being the next oldest, it became my responsibility to take care of my mother. I moved my mom to Bay City, so we could take care of her. My mother had already lost a sibling and now she was burying her own child. I wanted to do more with life because my brother was such a good person. I didn't want his life to go in vain. Before he died, I used to scream, yell and get stressed out about small things. Now I say, 'it's just spilled milk.' I've learned not to take life for granted or to get stressed about small things. When people complain about how difficult life is, I say 'This is the wrong place. Deal with it and move on.' This summer my family is taking a spur-of-the moment trip to San Francisco. We thought of it and we're doing it. My kids are flying for the first time, and we get to see a city that we've never been to. We used to plan, budget and wait for the perfect time. We would have thought of all the things to hold us back. Now we know there is no perfect time. We do things that we wouldn't do before, like going to a baseball game in the middle of the week. Don't put off enjoying life today to save money for when you get old, because you might not get old. Instead, enjoy every day."

Irma Pena, 46
Office Manager for Contractor
Bay City, Texas, United States

Go with the flow.

Remember you are just one small piece of the universe. The world does not revolve around you.

Vicky Scarth found herself experiencing "poor me" syndrome from time to time throughout life. When she took a trip to India, she realized that she was just a tiny piece of the universe. Vicky found that life was most beautiful when she just let herself go with the flow.

"Let things happen naturally. Reflect on why things happen the way they do and what lessons can be learned. India helped me embrace this concept. I went through some pretty horrible stuff in my life—I struggled with relationships, drugs, alcohol and perpetual sadness. When I got to India, I realized I was a small piece of the puzzle—very small. I learned that whatever I did, things would carry on as they were—not because I didn't matter, but because things are meant to happen in a certain way.

I still find life to be overwhelming, upsetting and very positive all at the same time, but knowing there is something greater than me—and that it'll all be all right in the end— helps me get through."

Vicky Scarth, 26
Case Worker for
Homeless People in Transition
London, United Kingdom

63 Never take significant others for granted.

Acknowledge the role your partner has played in helping you get to where you are today.

Ram Sah left Nepal in 1977 to begin a doctoral program at the University of California, Davis. His wife Devi and his children joined him in 1980. While Ram paved the path into society, Devi kept the family afloat with unconditional love and support.

"Devi's objective in life was not to ask for what she deserved. She didn't ask for equal rights. She sacrificed herself to make our family grow. That's the reason she holds such an important place in all of our hearts and we respect her so much. Devi's goal was to have the family excel and to give the children opportunities she didn't have, and she succeeded at that. She is our unsung hero. My sons and I are building a plaza of offices. We have decided to name it Devi Plaza, in honor of Devi. I have taught my sons to aim high, but stay low, to be humble no matter how much they accomplish. Being good, doing good things for others and helping whenever you have a chance will make you happy. Animals have mastered this. They will do anything to protect each other and make sacrifices to protect their young, but many humans still haven't caught on. Devi role-modeled this to our kids."

Ram Sah, PhD, 55
Retired Professor, & Entrepreneur
Davis, California, United States
(Originally from Janakpur, Nepal)

"I sacrificed a lot so my family could be here. When I got here, my husband was in graduate school, and I was trying to raise three boys. English was so hard, but I forced myself to learn it. I didn't care about speaking perfectly or about making mistakes, I just spoke. I used to wake up at 4:30 every morning and worked three jobs—I worked in a hospital, I did childcare and I took care of our boys. I never thought about myself. I was very involved with my kids—I made sure they studied and that they were well taken care of. My husband has a doctorate and two master's degrees, and I don't even have a formal education, but my kids never thought that I wasn't smart. I couldn't give my kids a lot of things, but they were happy with whatever they had. I taught our children to have a good heart, to mix with everybody no matter how smart or successful they were and to share whatever they had. Now, my kids are grown up and are all successful. I won't be free until they are all married and settled down. But then again, even my husband Ram needs me. I know he's bright, but he needs me. He's sloppy, he burns his food and he can't remember where he puts things. I could never leave him."

Devi Sah, 53
Full-Time Mom, Grandma, Wife & Part-Time
Daycare Provider
Davis, California, United States
(Originally from Janakpur, Nepal)

Don't get stressed about small things.

Instead, see stress as optional and opt out whenever possible.

Growing up in the beautiful yet conflict-stricken country of Uganda, Timothy Kiwala witnessed some atrocities that make him feel that it is unacceptable to get stressed or upset about small things.

"Every time I face a challenge, I remind myself that it could have been worse. I try to never get stressed out. I grew up in a war-ravaged coun-

try. I survived, and a lot of people died. This made me appreciate life. I know I am blessed to be alive.

We used to have road blocks, where officials would ask us for identification. When I was twelve, I rode in a caravan with a family, and I will never forget what I saw when we approached a checkpoint. The man in the van had forgotten his identifications at home. The guards asked him to sit down in the mud, and they beheaded him with an axe in front of his family and me. It's sad that children are growing up seeing this.

That memory stuck with me. I still get scared when I hear a bang on the door, or if someone sneaks up on me. But I will never let myself get stressed out about small stuff. I know that no matter how stressful something seems, it could always be worse. Besides, if you let yourself get stressed about small stuff, you will get old quickly. When life is overwhelming, remember that somewhere, someone else's life is more overwhelming."

Timothy Kiwala, 35
Graphic Artist
Kampala, Uganda

Empathizing with the World

Relating to people from all walks of life

65 Always stay open to all possibilities in life.
Although it's certain that life doesn't often go as planned, it continues to present us with endless possibilities waiting to be seized.

I had the privilege of crossing paths with Rebecca Walker in June 2006. As a bicultural, biracial woman who happens to be the daughter of Alice Walker, a mother, the author of several books and a visionary of third-wave feminism—making feminism accessible and inclusive to women from all walks of life—Rebecca believes that openness is an invaluable, sometimes underrated resource.

"Openness is our most precious human resource. With the view of openness, all things are possible: peace, strategies for global survival, greater intimacy with the people who rely on you for love and support and so on.

Openness goes beyond familiar ideas about tolerance and mutual understanding. In openness we reconnect with all the best qualities of our humanity: compassion, altruism, equanimity and, ultimately, freedom. These qualities do not belong to one race or religion, but to all of us.

Openness is not about being run over, used as a doormat or abused. Openness is about skillfully managing potential harm while safeguarding the beliefs that give you and the world the best chance for survival.

In the Buddhist tradition that I study, Vajrayana, great emphasis is placed on developing both openness and the protection of the openness. The teachings say that it is a mistake to think of these as separate or mutually exclusive.

Cultivating both simultaneously takes practice, but like any approach, the skill can be acquired through using the vast power of the mind and exercising discipline. I'll meet you there."

Rebecca Walker, 37
Writer & Activist
Honolulu, Hawaii, United States

66 Be in tune with your surroundings.

When out of your element or in a new environment, watch and learn from the social and cultural cues of those around you.

When Howard Thomas, a native of England, married a Panjabi woman with roots in Africa, he learned the importance of stepping back and blending in sometimes.

"When I'm in the U.K., in a context where English is the dominant language, I can give 100 percent of myself. When I'm with all of my wife's Panjabi relatives, whether I am in the U.K. or in Africa, I am more passive because I don't speak the language. I think it's important for families to be able to speak their native language with each other. If I were to impose a need to contribute to conversations, interrupt or ask for constant translations, I would break the natural flow. Instead, I just smile, go with the flow and take it all in."

Howard Thomas, 40
Sanitation Consultant
Birmingham, United Kingdom

Iksan Walhaidaya, originally from Indonesia, and Mahmudul Kabir, originally from Bangladesh, both wound up at Akita National University of Japan in the late 1990s and ended up making Japan their second home. Living in a ninety-nine percent homogeneous country, where they are forced to communicate, do business and study in their second language, has helped each of them learn intercultural diplomacy.

"When I came here five years ago, I didn't understand any Japanese. I took an intensive class in Shinjiku, Tokyo, and then came to Akita to begin graduate school. There is only one other student here from Indonesia, but lots of Malays (whose language is very similar to my native language), and lots of other international students. Sometimes, I'm a different person when I'm with my Malaysian friends than I am with my Japanese friends. In my culture, we tell lots of jokes and sometimes tease each other. It's sometimes hard for my Japanese friends to understand why I think something is funny. When I'm with my Japanese friends, I've learned to laugh on cue and be a little careful with the jokes I tell, because we have a different sense of humor. Even though I've had to adjust a lot, I'm glad I came here. If I hadn't left Indonesia, I wouldn't have had the chance to learn about cultural differences or know what other parts of the world were like."

Iksan Walhidaya, 25
Graduate Student
Akita, Japan
(Originally from Jakarta, Indonesia)

"I came to Japan six years ago. It was really hard. I was the only Bangladeshi, and I never got a chance to speak my native language, and I didn't know where I fit in. Now I think I'm lucky. I think in Japanese, my gestures have become Japanese and I have the chance to speak with a lot of Japanese people. I've learned so much since coming here. Now, after seeing the quality of life in Japan and a fast-changing society, it will be a little sad to go back to Bangladesh, where not much has changed."

Mahmudul Kabir, 26
Graduate Student
Akita, Japan
(Originally from Dhaka, Bangladesh)

67 Empathize, don't sympathize.

Empathizing helps us imagine what it's like to walk in the shoes of others and enables us to see the world from other perspectives. Sympathizing makes others feel and operate like victims.

Aster Awaji fell in love with the man who is now her husband, when he was doing a year of volunteer service in Aster's hometown in Africa. Aster left her upper-class family behind to begin a new life and start her own family in Akita, Japan with her husband. After arriving in Japan, Aster learned Japanese and opened an Ethiopian restaurant in an attempt to share her culture. She is committed to teaching her children to value all parts of their identity—both the African and the Japanese.

"My son looks a lot like my husband, but my daughter looks a lot like me, so sometimes people call her a 'gaijin' (foreigner) when they see her. When she asks me why she is black and why people call her a gaijin, I explain to her that she is partially black because her mom is black. I want my children to be proud of who they are, not feel sorry for themselves."

Aster Awaji, 35
Restaurant Owner
Akita, Japan
(Originally from Ethiopia)

Norma Lopez is the daughter of Mexican immigrants. Norma's father was one of sixteen children, while her mother was one of eight. Neither of her parents had the opportunity to finish high school, as they were needed at home to help support their families. Imagining the world through the eyes of her parents helped Norma learn how to empathize with others.

"I learned the value of empathy at a young age. My parents often called on me to translate, write letters and make phone calls. I often missed out on being with people my own age, going to friends' homes after school and going to birthday parties. The ability to empathize allowed me to see the world through my parents' eyes and saved me from becoming resentful. I was not a perfect child. I sometimes got angry with my parents for telling me that I was not allowed to accept an invitation to play. As a teen, I felt like I could never do anything fun. But I always understood the difficulties my parents faced. I knew that the world was a challenging place for my parents. My parents faced injustice on a daily basis as they navigated outside their home. I'm positive that they have many stories of humiliation and marginalization that I've never heard.

Without taking time to step back and examine your relationships and the situations you get into with your loved ones, it becomes very easy to build unnecessary resentment. It's just easier to let things go. How many people do you know who still blame their parents for things they didn't accomplish in life? I'm sure they are not very introspective or empathetic people."

Norma Lopez, 35
Social Worker
Berkeley, California, United States
(Originally from Mexico)

121

68 Find commonality with everyone you encounter.

No matter how different you are on the surface, you're bound to have something in common.

Six-year-old Pavan might be too young to fully understand what the word "commonality" means, but he's already figured out how to befriend classmates and neighborhood children of all backgrounds.

"There's just one Nepali in my class, and that's me. I have two Mexican friends, a white friend and a Chinese friend. All of our families are a little bit the same. I want to go to Nepal someday. I like to learn about Nepal from my grandfather—he knows most, but my mom knows a little bit too. I know that houses are built out of wood and there are lots of fish, rice, soup, dhal and tomatoes in Nepal. There are mango trees and jungles and lots of dust. Someday when my little brother Deepak grows up, I'll go see Nepal."

Pavan, 6
Kindergartner
Davis, California, United States

Juana Ojeda left Mexico in 1995 to start a new life in Oakland, California. She wanted to learn English and she wanted to experience life on her own, independent of her father. Since coming to the United States, not only has Juana grown as a person, she has also learned how to connect with people of all backgrounds.

"Learning to accept different cultures has enriched my life. In my hometown, everyone was one color. Here, there are so many colors, cultures and different kinds of people. I've learned that it doesn't matter how different you are from others, you can always find at least one thing you have in common or one thing you can both relate to. In life, some people are monetarily wealthy—they have a lot and don't know what to do with it. Other people are successful—they live freely and enjoy life without caring about what others think about them.

I'm happy about all the immigration issues that are going on in the United States right now and impressed with the way all of us immigrants are pulling together. Immigrants deserve rights in the U.S. We pay taxes, spend our money and put our money back into the economy. We should be acknowledged. No matter what the laws say, this is my home and I will be here. My dream is to own my own business, be my own boss and visit my family whenever I feel like it."

Juana Ojeda, 32
Chef
Oakland, California, United States
(Originally from Acapulco, Mexico)

69

Never impose your ideologies on others or assume that your way is better.
Instead, look for common ground.

Anna Adams, a Catholic campus minister, strives to inspire others to approach religion in a broad manner.

"Imposing ideologies on others or trying to handle religion in a black-and-white way is a discredit to God, and an insult. It alienates others, rather than nurturing spirituality.

The holy spirit is present in the wisdom of many of the world's religions. It's the same spirit that inspires us all. Humans have an innate need to connect with others and connect with God. There's a lot that unites us. We have more to learn from each other than we have to fight about. It's our job as people of faith to affirm that in each other, rather than tear it down."

Anna Adams, 32
Campus Minister
Cottonwood, California, United States

After September 11, 2001, Amina Khan was disheartened by the way her religion was being represented in the media. Amina's gut instinct was that people of different faiths and religious backgrounds should have the easiest time envisioning the world through each other's lenses because of their common belief in a higher being. By hosting and participating in interfaith dialogues, Amina has successfully constructed bridges between people with vastly different belief systems.

"The media and public-relations campaign against Islam and Muslims that emerged from the ashes of 9/11 made me realize that as a Muslim, I could not stay silent while my faith was being typecasted as one of violence and anger. I started speaking to people about faith and found that people were thirsty for knowledge about Islam and Muslims and open to learning about the commonalities of faith.

Imagining the world through the eyes of someone else with a different belief system is much like putting yourself in someone else's shoes. I firmly believe that imagining the world through the eyes or soul of a different belief system is easier than imagining oneself to be a different race, or of a different economic status. Why? Because belief systems are fundamentally the same. All those who believe in a specific religion have already made the leap of faith. We all believe in a higher being, in our time on this earth being limited, on a certain set of values that are considered to be "divinely" passed down. A very wealthy person (might struggle to) imagine himself or herself to be part of the disenfranchised poor, just as a resident of Washington, D.C. might find it difficult to imagine what it's like to be Sudanese. There are no common links there, but those who believe have common links."

Amina Khan, 37
Attorney
Washington, D.C., United States
(Originally from Pakistan)

125

70

Respect other cultural and religious aesthetics and practices.

It is not your place to decide what is appropriate for other people.

Hayfa Ahmad is a strong, motivated Muslim woman from Doha, Qatar. In such a complex world, Hayfa thinks people shouldn't get caught up on judging each other's cultural and religious apparel and practices.

"It is one of our Islamic rules that a woman should cover herself, not to be like a big rubbish bag, like some people think, but as a sign of modesty. In Islam, we (women) can wear whatever we want, as long as it covers our bodies in a proper way. Wearing the hijab makes me feel safer. Having your hair or your body exposed can make you feel vulnerable. For all women, freedom is not about showing your body; freedom is a state of mind. I wear whatever I want when I am with other women and children. Sometimes, when I wear fitted clothes that cover my body but show my body's definition, I feel like men look at me in an annoying way. When I wear an abaiya or looser-fitting clothes, I feel more free and liberated. Nobody has their eyes on me or sees me as sexy. They see me for me. I feel free to do whatever I would like. Sometimes, I want to feel that way. Life is too short, so we should enjoy it. People in the East and the West need to learn how to respect and be nice to each other. This verse in the Qu'ran best describes why it is important for us to respect each other's traditions, practices and choices."

Bismilla'hir-Rahma'nir-Raheem

"O disbelievers,
I do not worship what you worship.
Nor are you worshippers of what I worship.
Nor will I be a worshipper of what you worship.
Nor will you be worshippers of what I worship.
For you is your religion, and for me is my religion."

Hayfa Ahmad, 25
Web Designer
Doha, Qatar

126

As an Afghani-Muslim woman married to a Caucasian-Jewish man, living in the San Francisco Bay Area, Latifa Popal believes respect for all persons, regardless of background, is invaluable.

"I have chosen to take a little bit of everything, Western and Eastern philosophy, and combine them into one. If we're going to be in a global environment, we shouldn't judge each other on the types of clothing we wear, the color of our skin, our ethnicity or our religion. Afghanistan has become known as a place of illiteracy and oppression, but it wasn't always like that. War has caused those conditions.

Below the surface, we are all humans. There is a real beauty to having different people together in one environment. We get the benefit of beautiful food and many different perspectives. What does it mean if we refer to each other as 'evil?' First, we're people. Look below the surface and you'll see layers of beauty and positivity. Once you strike a friendship with an Afghan person, you'll have a friendship that will last a lifetime."

Latifa Popal, 38
Registrar & Activist
San Francisco, California, United States
(Originally from Kabul, Afghanistan)

Treat others as they'd like to be treated, not as you'd like to be treated.

Don't take up a cause without understanding the implications your cause has on people.

Semya Hakim is a professor at St. Cloud State University in Minnesota. She challenges xenophobia, sexism and racism on a daily basis.

"The decision to wear a hijab or a burkha is like women ourselves—varied and complex. When non-Muslims focus on Muslim women covering themselves, it suggests that Muslim women are not active agents in our own lives. It also detracts from larger systemic issues such as anti-Muslim bias, racism and actual forms of sexism that may exist in Muslim communities. By focusing on burkhas and hijabs, society objectifies Muslim women. The discussion often leads others to equate the entire personhood of a Muslim woman by her veil or lack of a veil. Like all women, Muslim women are multi-dimensional and should not be defined by one choice.

My life is affected greatly by stereotypes of Muslims and of Arabs. Having other folks' perceptions of me not match up to my perception of myself is sometimes exhausting. Because I am an Arab woman, non-Arabs don't know what box to put me in racially. I feel like I always have to be on guard. To know that I can be turned into a spokesperson for Islam without my consent, to constantly be asked to explain Muslim ideology or advocate on behalf of Muslim students takes up a lot of time and energy. What could I do with this energy in a different type of world? On one hand, living in a society where anti-Arab racism and Islamophobic bias are prevalent has made me a stronger person. At the end of the day, though, I would not want to be anyone else.

The most challenging part of being a woman is facing sexism and knowing that some people will never believe that women should be treated equally to men. The most rewarding part of being a woman is the other women. They allow me to make mistakes, grow, change and ultimately become a better woman."

Semya Hakim, PhD, 39
Lebanese-American Professor
Minneapolis, Minnesota, United States

Envision the world from the perspectives of others.

This will make you a more compassionate person.

Although Thanuja Kulasekera has never visited the Tamil region of her country, studying abroad helped her develop a sense of empathy for Tamils in Sri Lanka.

"I studied at the University of Wisconsin and at St. Cloud State University in Minnesota. Being in the U.S. helped me understand what it's like to be a second- or third-class citizen in another country and gave me perspective about the conflict in my own country. I could only begin to understand how minorities in Sri Lanka would feel, being treated as second-class citizens in their own country. I knew someday I could come back to a country I could call my own, where I would be treated as a first-class citizen.

We need to accept and respect the needs and differences of all ethnicities, be it Tamil, Singhalese, Muslim, Burgher or others, because Sri Lanka is that. Until we learn to accept each other as Sri Lankans, we will fail, as a country, to let peace prevail."

Thanuja, Kulasekera, 29
Information-Technology Consultant
Colombo, Sri Lanka

ian Tamil Tigers of Elam. Letchumanan worries about the kind of life his students will be able to lead in the war-impacted region of Sri Lanka.

"When I envision the world through the eyes of my students, I get worried. It will be difficult for them to bring children into this world. I still remember what it was like to be a student. When I was in seventh grade in 1983, riots happened in Colombo, and many Tamil homes were destroyed and looted. Between 1991 and 1995, when I was a college student in Jaffna, everything was very expensive—kerosene was around 300 rupees. Food was expensive; there were shellings and bombings. Transportation was cut off. There were no bicycles in the streets, very few cars and lots of checkpoints.

Thirty-three-year-old Letchumanan Kirupairthnam, is a Christian Brother and an English teacher in the Tamil village of Wanni, Sri Lanka. When I crossed his path in 2003, he shared the struggles that he and his students faced on a daily basis. Each day, Letchumanan commuted twelve miles by motorbike from Mannar to the village of Wanni. Along the way, he passed signs posted by UNICEF, reminding him of the presence of explosives and land mines; and was required to stop at two checkpoints—one for the Singhalese army and one for the Libertar-

After the military actions, we had suicide bombers. It was very sad. Some people lost their loved ones and felt there was nothing left for them. They were willing to sacrifice themselves to bring independence and freedom, and help others.

We need to meet the fundamental needs of the people in the northeast, resettle displaced people, create housing and quality education. We need a separate state to accommodate all the Muslims and Tamils. Right now, there's no free elections, and many people can't vote. Singhalese and Tamils need to stop blaming each other and start trusting each other. My dream is that people will come here (to the northern region of Sri Lanka) without being afraid, and have a good opinion of Tamils, and the military will be gone. We will be able to protect and keep our cultural values."

Letchumanan Kirupairthnam, 35
English Teacher & Christian Brother
Mannar, Sri Lanka
(Originally from Jaffna, Sri Lanka)

These are displaced Tamil children who study in the village of Wanni. Their school was destroyed as a result of the ongoing ethnic conflict between Tamils and Singhalese, but they continue to study under tarps set up in the sand.

Nearly all of the 450 students at Wanni school have been displaced and forced to exchange the comforts of their homes to spend time refugee camps in Madu, a village about fifty kilometers away. Since returning to the village, military personal and checkpoints have become a regular component of everyday scenery.

73   Learn a second or a third language.

Speaking a second language is like having a second soul. It gives you another lens to view life through.

Speaking several languages has given Vinay Joosery the privilege of intimately experiencing cultures throughout the world.

"I have had the chance to live and study in countries throughout the world. I speak Mauritian Creole, English, French and Swedish. Speaking the language of the country I'm in brings me closer to the culture and the people of the country. Traveling the world and learn-

ing new languages has helped me view the world as one big nation, rather than thinking in terms of 'us and them.' We are all on the same boat."

Vinay Joosery, 33
Sales Manager
Beau-Bassin, Mauritius

Claudia Ramos became bilingual at a young age and served as the social link between her family and mainstream United States.

"I came from Mexico when I was three. When I started school, a whole new world opened up for me. As soon as I entered my bilingual kindergarten program, I realized I had to learn English to live in the world I was living in.

At home, my parents only spoke Spanish, and made it a rule that we could not speak English at home. I had to grow up fast. I was the most fluent English speaker and a full-time translator for my family. I translated at doctors' appointments, I ordered in restaurants and went to parent-teacher conferences with my parents. I still remember my fourth-grade parent-teacher conference. My mom asked me to translate and ask the teacher how my English was doing. She asked the teacher to speculate about why I seemed shy when it came to translating for my family. The teacher replied that it was because I was only nine. I felt a lot of pressure having such a big responsibility.

Because I speak two languages, I have two cultures and a lot of opportunity to accomplish something in this world. Spanish is my native language that keeps me in touch with my culture, my roots and who I am. Speaking English has given me a lot of opportunities and opened a lot of doors for me. It allowed me to travel, to go to college and have an open mind about the world. I feel lucky to have those opportunities, while keeping my roots intact. The world would be great if everyone maintained their native language and learned one more. It's great to learn a new language and culture if you have the chance, but always keep your own close to your heart."

Claudia Ramos, 22
Student
Lindsay, California, United States
(Originally from Cheran, Mexico)

74 Listen more and talk less.
It's the best way to learn.

As a Catholic Indian raised in the Middle East, Ajay Jose credits listening as the most important cultural link. Ajay was born in Kerala, India and moved to Bahrain at the age of eight. Because his parents were determined to give him a quality Catholic education, he switched schools a total of eight times by the time he reached twelfth grade. As a result, Ajay has learned the value of listening and learning from his environment.

"The more you listen, the more you learn and the more you evolve. I have learned from asking questions, prompting others to talk and then listening. If I try to preempt a conversation with my own thoughts, I might take the conversation in a wrong way or jump to wrong conclusions. When you listen to others, you show them that you respect them. Once you establish respect, you feel less threatened and can have a better conversation. Listening shows that you respect the other's time, opinions and the person. It allows you the chance to empathize. When you listen, you will realize that the other person's concerns are the same as yours. It aids in understanding the situation in a sharper way; you can come up with solutions that will aid both of you."

Ajay Jose, 32
Engineer
Manana, Bahrain
(Originally from Kerala, India)

Have faith in others.

Given the opportunity, everyone has the potential to do good.

Sister Ann Manthey thought sisterhood would be the best way for her to make a difference. Through her vocation, Sister Ann learned to have faith in everyone.

"I took my vows to become a Catholic sister in 1946. I know that some people in society don't think of sisters as normal women. People struggle to understand why we would choose to commit to celibacy, service and sisterhood for our whole lives. But when I look at society and celebrities, I can see the idea of service is catching on, and people are realizing that there is satisfaction in giving back and serving others. That gives me hope that the world is becoming a better place. As a sister, I realize it is sometimes hard for clergymen to accept the ideas of women. It's sometimes frustrating, but we do what we can from within the system. Just as men and women bring different gifts to families, they bring different gifts to the church. I've learned that people are really good. Sometimes people get caught in a bad environment and make bad decisions. But we can believe in others, plant a seed for them. The seed might not germinate until they're forty, fifty or sixty years old, but they'll remember that someone had faith in them along the way. I still do get frus-

trated with people sometimes, but I am happy knowing that I have done what I could to try and help. Every lifestyle has its ups and downs, but we need to accept the difficult moments to be who we truly are. I've been a sister for more than sixty years and I wouldn't trade it all for the world. What good would love be if it wasn't given freely?"

Sister Ann Manthey, 80
Director of Religious Education
Whitehall, Wisconsin, United States

135

76 Stay connected.

Never isolate or alienate yourself from the society you live in.

Photo by Christine Johnson

When I met Michael Moore in February 2002, he had already released *Bowling for Columbine*, and was in the process of creating *Fahrenheit 9/11* and publishing *Stupid White Men*. He has since released *Sicko* (2007), in which he addresses the inaccessibility of American health care. Michael Moore points out that most Americans do not know who the top people in office are or what the largest American corporation is, and fewer than half of all U.S. citizens vote. He believes Americans need to be less apathetic and more in touch. It is this belief, coupled with passion, that gives Michael the drive to be a filmmaker, an author and an activist. Michael Moore started his activism career when he was a senior in high school after learning that he only needed twenty signatures to run for public office. Michael gave it a shot, ran for school board and became the first eighteen-year-old old to get elected to a public office in the United States. Today Michael is a voice for people are not heard. He challenges everyone to vote, know who's calling the shots and stay in touch with mainstream society.

"Don't separate yourselves from the world you live in. Listen to the music people listen to, and watch the programs people watch. Before you can make any sort of change, you have to learn how to connect with people."

Michael Moore, 52
Film Director, Author & Activist
Flint, Michigan, United States

See the world in all shades of gray.

Most issues in life are complex. Looking for one black-and-white answer may leave you feeling disempowered.

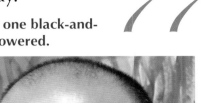

As a gay, fair-skinned Latino, Ivan Pagan knows the priceless value of seeing the world in all shades of gray.

"Great loss happens when people try to see the world in black-and-white terms. I come from a multiplicity of experiences, identities and struggles. I was born in Puerto Rico, spent some time in Argentina and eventually worked my way to the United States. Culturally, I feel like I'm a little bit of this and a little bit of that. In some ways, I feel like I can navigate culture, almost invisibly. I'm fair-skinned, so when I speak English, people assume I'm white. When I speak Spanish, people assume I'm Latino. When I speak English, I find that I'm more rigid and speak more from the mind. When I speak Spanish, I'm more fluid and speak more from the heart. I have used my ability to navigate culture to my advantage. Within the dominant Latino community, the queer experience is not readily accepted or talked about. I gained strength for dealing with that part of my identity in the white culture, while I was living and working in Madison, Wisconsin. When I moved to the West Coast, I merged my identities as queer and Latino. Now, when I'm in the right space and feel comfortable, I can identify as a gay Latino.

People come in all shapes, sizes, spirits and colors. If you try to oversimplify the world and see everything in black and white, that's all you'll ever get. A perfect world would be filled with acceptance, access to other languages and ways of thinking, and compassion. That's what would break down black-and-white thinking."

Ivan Pagan, 41
Educator & Community Activist
Lafayette, California, United States
(Originally from Mayaguez, Puerto Rico)

137

78 Break unhealthy cycles and habits.

Heal and create new, healthy cycles that are based on love and respect.

Paulette Fox-Beardsley is determined not to let the hardships and loss she has experienced affect her own children. She is breaking the cycle.

"I've witnessed a lot of things in my short life. My dad was an alcoholic and had a chemical imbalance. One of my brothers drank himself to death and another one hasn't spoken to me for years. My first marriage was unhealthy and abusive. It took me seven years to leave, but I finally did it.

Now, I have a wonderful husband and two wonderful children. I feel so lucky that sometimes I want to pinch myself. I learned at a young age that you have to have faith that things will be okay. If our family life is unhealthy, we can either let it consume us, or we can move on and break the cycle. Breaking the cycle is a challenge, but I know I can't go back. My kids have no idea what I've been through, so I am writing memoirs of my life to share with them.

I really believe we all have to have a light that shines—something that makes us glow, that connects us to the world. I write, I have a green belt in karate, and I make jewelry. In 2005, my husband and I opened a coffeeshop called Alternative Ground, here in a town of 1,500. Our goal was to enable natives of Whitehall to see and experience the world through a different lens."

Paulette Fox-Beardsley, 48
Coffeeshop Owner
Whitehall, Wisconsin, United States

Reciprocating

Mastering the art of giving, taking
and appreciating

Be reciprocal.

Humans crave reciprocity in all social interactions. Remember you have as much to gain from the resiliency of others as they have to gain from you.

Adeel Hasan left his comfort zone in Montreal, Canada for a job in Doha, Qatar. While in Qatar, Adeel found his niche, befriending other expatriates from Palestine, India and Pakistan, as well as other Qataris. Being reciprocal has helped him feel at home away from home.

"Never expect anything from others until you actually put in work yourself. Meeting and greeting others from all over the world has been nothing but a pleasure and a privilege for me. I meet simple people who don't have much, but actually have so much to teach people like me. Reality only kicks in when you leave your natural surroundings."

Adeel Hasan, 30
Entrepreneur
Doha, Qatar
(Originally from Montreal, Canada)

Be inclusive.

Strive to never make anyone feel left out.

Bob Kokott remembers countless gatherings around his Polish grandmother's humble kitchen table in North Creek, Wisconsin. Bob's grandmother embedded the concept of inclusivity in Bob's head from a young age with her saying, "C'mon in, pull up another chair, there's always room for one more." This group of college students grasps the concept, as they manage to squeeze twenty people into a human cinnamon roll-style group hug.

"There's always room for one more at the table. Why? Because what holds us together is our recognition of the vulnerability of each and every human heart."

Bob Kokott, 43
Massage Therapist, Teacher & Dancer
Minneapolis, Minnesota, United States
(Originally from Madison, Wisconsin)

81

Use your birthday as an opportunity to count your blessings and as an excuse to let others know how much you appreciate them.

In the craziness of life, it's sometimes hard to keep up with everyone's birthday and easy to feel sorry for yourself as you realize that you are getting older. Instead, use your birthday as a time to let friends, family, co-workers and acquaintances know how much you appreciate having them in your life.

When Tarne Padhaal turned fifty, he invited his friends and family from the United States, Europe and other parts of Africa to join him in Kampala, Uganda for a huge birthday bash.

"My family is spread all over the world. I really wanted to see everyone, so I thought the best thing to do would be to throw a party, invite them all to Uganda and let them all experience this country. I will do the same thing again when I turn sixty. I don't eat alone."

Tarne Padhaal, 50
Engineer
Kampala, Uganda

Commit random acts of kindness whenever you have a chance.

82

Give spare change to homeless people without second-guessing how they will use the money. When you're in a restaurant, rather than throwing away leftover food, neatly package it and give it to someone who is hungry. If you have nothing to give, offer a smile and a greeting.

Allean Ross is a college-educated woman and a mother with experience working in the computer-science field. After being diagnosed with post-traumatic stress disorder, her life shifted. Still, the physically frail Allean keeps a resilient spirit, as she returns to the streets of Oakland day after day to politely offer passers-by the chance to purchase a newspaper.

"I've learned to take things one day at a time, because life doesn't always turn out the way you want it to. People let each other down a lot, so you should trust in God. I went to college in Washington D.C., got a degree in computer science and worked in the field for a long time. I was diagnosed with post-traumatic stress disorder, and now I'm here. I never planned to be on the street selling the *Street Sheet* to get enough money to survive, but life doesn't always work out the way you want it to. The best part of my life is that I get to talk to all kinds of people all day long. If you have the chance to help someone else out, you should, because you could be wearing the same shoes one day."

Allean Ross, 57
Mother
Oakland, California, United States

143

83   Appreciate sisters and brothers.

Siblings know everything about us and love us anyways.

Makoto Urano was raised in a single-parent family in Osaka, Japan and always dreamed about having a sister or a brother. When Makoto became an adult, his dream came true.

"I loved my mom, but I always wished I could have a brother or sister. Whenever I saw other children hanging out with their siblings after school or during summer break, I prayed that I could have one too. I used to imagine what it would be like to have a sister or brother and think about what we would do for fun. When I turned nineteen, it happened. I learned that I had a brother living in my same city. My mother and father had split up when I was a baby. I went with my mother and my brother stayed with my father. My mom waited to tell me until she thought I was old enough to understand. After being apart for so long, my brother feels more like a friend than a sibling. We would have had to spend our childhood together to fully appreciate each other as brothers, but there is something nice about just knowing that I have a brother."

Makoto Urano, 31
Sales Consultant
Osaka, Japan

Kavita and Ganeev came to California with their parents as political refugees in 2003. As their family has carved its niche in the U.S., these two siblings have been inseparable.

"I try to do stuff good, so my brother can follow my footsteps. If I don't behave, he won't. If I behave nicely, Ganeev will copy me. When he's hurt, I help him. I also try to help him with his homework when my mom is cooking. When my brother is lonely, we play and try and come up with interesting games. Sometimes we pretend that we are having an Indian wedding—my brother pretends to be the bride and I am his sister. My brother is my biggest champion on earth and will be until I die."

"When someone is mean to me, my sister Kavita makes a face at the person so they will leave me alone. Sometimes she gets mad at me when I pull her hair. When I push her, she says stop!! But I love having a sister because she always helps me and plays with me. I like to sleep next to her sometimes, so I can play with her hair. I love my sister forever."

Kavita, 10 & Ganeev, 7
Siblings
Walnut Creek, California United States
(Originally from Kisumu, Kenya)

84 Always give others the benefit of the doubt.

When you take a risk and believe in others, they are more likely to believe in themselves and perform well. When you doubt others, you are likely reinforcing the self-doubt they already have.

Nicole Jackson, a native of East Oakland, California, was in culture shock when she landed at an isolated, upper-class, mostly white, Catholic campus just over the hill from home. Nicole doubted that she would ever find her niche and was ready to give up, until she encountered a professor who refused to give up on her.

"Jeanine King was the first African-American teacher I had at my college, and the last. She was young and energetic. Like me, she was trying to find her place, as it was her first year. We just kind of clicked. In her class, I got to study things that were relevant to who I was and where I came from. Jeanine definitely gave me the benefit of the doubt. When I didn't come to class or I turned things in late, rather than giving up on me, she would get on my case. She always made it clear that she knew I would get the work done and that it would be good. Jeanine seemed sure that I would end up all right and that what I needed was a friend, rather than an authority figure.

If I hadn't met Jeanine, I might have dropped out of college. Jeanine inspired me to explore women's studies courses. This ultimately led me on a path to meeting other amazing faculty members and friends. It helped me develop a natural support network and helped me find my place."

Nicole Jackson, 22
African History Graduate Student
Columbus, Ohio, United States
(Originally from Oakland, California)

Jeanine King is paying it forward, when she gives her students the benefit of the doubt.

"I can easily allow students the benefit of the doubt because I was the grateful recipient of the benefit. Affirmative action, the time and commitment of my overworked teachers and the hope of my poverty-line community gave me a chance. I know that each student that walks into my classroom carries enormous possibility. It is both a disservice to the student and a loss to the community of scholars to miss out on encouraging this potential and the transformation that an education should promise.

I grew up in the projects with uneducated parents who were the children of sharecroppers. Although my father never had a chance to pursue a formal education, he was obsessed with his children's education. Self-taught, he loved to read and was optimistic about the possibilities for our futures. This inspired me to earn a doctorate degree at UC. Berkeley. I was also influenced by the high expectations of a teacher and mentor who couldn't have been more different than me. She was the first teacher who refused to accept my excuses. She presented academic excellence as a challenge she believed I could meet, and I rose to it. When I was in a college women's studies class taught by radical feminist Gloria Anzaldua, I was part of an emotional battle between the women of color and white women. Gloria talked about the possibility of being bridges to one another. We shouted that bridges get run over, walked on. She said that bridges hold up, bring together. She said that in order to be a teacher, you must be a bridge. I never forgot that lesson—it affirms my essential beliefs about the role of a teacher. We have the duty to use our experiences and knowledge as a mode of passage for our students. This encompassing and rewarding endeavor leaves no room for doubt."

Jeanine King, 38
Women's Studies & English Professor
San Francisco, California, United States

85 Be generous.

Be kind with your words, take time to listen and share without looking for something in return.

As an only child who never had the opportunity to share with siblings, it took Adil Colabawala until adulthood to learn the value of sharing.

"I am an only child. I grew up feeling like I was the center of the world. I have a friend that inspired me to think about things in a broader perspective. He taught me to get beyond me, me, me and I, I, I. Once when we were hanging out, someone asked me for a cigarette. Even though I had a full box, I said 'no.' My friend then handed the guy one of his cigarettes without thinking twice. My friend told me that the pleasure you get from sharing is unexplainable. The next time I had the chance to share, I did. The guy smiled and said 'thank you,' and I felt so good. I had to realize that the world is not just about me. It's about what surrounds me."

Adil Colabawala, 22
Biochemistry Student
Northridge, California, United States
(Originally from Mumbai, India)

Jane Camarillo was born in Texas in 1957 to a Japanese mother and a Latino father. She remembers not quite fitting neatly into any category and sometimes feeling impatient with her parents. While pursuing a doctorate in social psychology, Jane discovered the field of college student affairs and never looked back. Reflecting on her childhood interactions with her parents has ultimately inspired Jane to be more present and generous with the college students she works with.

"If I had a daughter, I would urge her to be generous with love, optimism, time, forgiveness and all the human resources that can be shared. When I was a rebelling teenager, I remember thinking that my time was too valuable to spend explaining things to my parents. So instead, there was silence between us. As an adult, I began to regret the time that I lost as a result of being stubborn and decided to make a conscious effort to be more generous with the individuals I interacted with.

When I embarked on my career in college student affairs, I had a conversation with a graduating senior. The senior told me that I was responsible for where he was now. The student had been in trouble on several occasions and was accustomed to hearing 'Here is the rule you broke, and here is your punishment.' I had spent time explaining why a policy existed, how it was relevant to him and how the experiences he was enduring were a test of character. The student told me that he appreciated that I didn't treat him like a jerk, that I took a few minutes to give him context. I learned that you just never know when someone's life might change for the better, because you slowed down, took time and approached a situation with the attitude of generosity."

Jane Camarillo, 50
College Vice-Provost
Lafayette, California, United States
(Originally from San Antonio, Texas)

86 Never take small things for granted.
We can learn an infinite amount from the innocence of the world's smallest beings.

Aun Ali Khalfan has been publishing the English version of the Qu'ran for decades to promote peace and understanding. In 2007, Aun invested in one of the world's youngest authors—his grandson.

"Children are one step ahead of us. They learn faster than adults and have so much to teach adults—they have the capacity to learn up to seven languages between the ages of three and eleven. They are loving, caring and have an honest way of dealing with the world. Children speak the truth, while adults are sometimes afraid to do that. My religion teaches that children should be treated as kings during their first seven years of life, as trainees for the next seven so they can be guided and taught, and as the boss when they are between the ages of seven and fourteen. If the world was run by children rather than grown-ups, it would be such an innocent place. I have high hopes for my grandchildren's generation. They'll do better. There will be no war."

Aun Ali Khalfan, 63
Publisher of Qu'ran
Franklin Square, New York, United States
(Originally from Madagascar, Africa)

87 Live every day to the fullest with no regrets.
Take risks, forgive, say "I love you" and say "goodbye."

Erin Sanders often didn't see eye to eye with her father as she grew up. Her father's job sometimes required him to be away from home for as long as five days at a time. Erin couldn't help but feel resentful. When Erin turned sixteen, her father died unexpectedly, and she never had a chance to say goodbye.

"Losing my dad changed my perception of relationships and life in general. I realized that my dad sacrificed a lot so he could send me to a nice school, so my mom could be a stay-at-home mom, and so our family could have a comfortable life. I learned how unpredictable life is and realized that it's not worth sweating the small stuff. I learned the importance of forgiving and saying 'I love you.' I regretted not telling my dad that I loved him. Now, I never go to bed mad. I never end a conversation with my siblings, my mom or my boyfriend without saying 'I love you.'

When I was a senior in high school, I learned that my best friend Renee had terminal brain cancer. She died one month after we graduated. Renee knew death was coming and accepted it in a positive way. She was stronger than the rest of us. To this day, whenever I'm down and out, I think about Renee and my dad, and hope that they are watching over me. Today when I see a husband and a wife, a father and a daughter together or a few good friends hanging out, I think of my dad and Renee. I appreciate everything, and I cherish all the relationships in my life.

If you feel something for someone and you don't express it, it's selfish. You should never assume that someone knows how you feel. It takes a strong person to be vulnerable. Put aside differences, forgive others, say, 'I love you' whenever you have the chance. Even if the effort is not reciprocated, you'll know that you did your part."

Erin Sanders, 23
Insurance Salesperson
San Ramon, California, United States

Universal Truths
to Live by

88 Appreciate the simple things in life.

Happiness is not the result of material goods.

In June 2001, I prepared to visit Cuba as a journalist and graduate student. At the time, I worked for a small paper in St. Joseph, Minnesota, as I was finishing my master's degree in social responsibility at St. Cloud State University. The U.S. Treasury department denied my visa, however. Thankfully a peace and justice organization took me in and added me to their group visa. Upon arriving in Cuba, I found a country filled with people who had embraced the concept of simplicity. It's true—the cars are decades old; children play with handmade toys and use boards to stay afloat in the ocean on scorching hot days; most people have simple homes; and no one is extremely rich. Yet people persevere and live life in a vibrant, colorful and musical way. Although far from perfect, there is something charming about a country, that in spite of having a scarcity of products due to the U.S.-imposed embargo, provides its citizens with free healthcare, free education, food and housing. One afternoon, I crossed paths with the man the world agrees to either love or hate—the now former leader, Fidel Castro.

"I'm concerned about the overflow of advertisements in the U.S. teaching people to look for happiness in goods that they don't have the means to obtain. We live in a world where seventy percent of the people do not know how to read or write, where four-fifths of the people are malnourished and where five percent of the people use twenty-five percent of the world's resources. If everyone in China decided to consume resources at that rate, we'd have a global crisis.

We, Cubans, have had to survive in a struggle with the superpower for over forty years. Regarding me, I can tell you that the President of the United States has more power. I am not myself, I am one of many people. We've been isolated in a utopia, and today intelligence and talent are in the masses. I'd like all Americans to be able to come here, so we can show them what we've done for mankind. I hope everyone can be trained in the idea of loving life, otherwise we'll become nothing more than pets in cages."

Fidel Castro, 74
Leader of Cuba
Havana, Cuba

Be humble.

Humility keeps you in touch with the most important aspects of life.

Artie Lee Dawkins can most often be found on Piedmont Avenue in Oakland, California, selling the *Street Sheet* (the newspaper sold by homeless people throughout the San Francisco Bay Area). Although life didn't turn out for Artie the way he had hoped, he credits his grandmother with giving him the strength to pull through.

"My grandmother taught me everything I know. She taught me how to survive, how to live and how to learn. Now I sell *Street Sheet*s to survive. I've had a hard life, but I'm hanging in there."

Artie Lee Dawkins, 66
Street Sheet *Newspaper Vendor*
Oakland, California, United States

Five-year-old Tamanna, the daughter of a servant in Calcutta, India, reminds us all of the value of humility.

"I have three brothers and a mom. We sleep in different places on different nights. Last night we slept on the balcony veranda of the cinema hall. We usually eat out because there's no place to cook, but I don't mind 'cause I like to eat out. When I grow up, I'll be a doctor, 'cause my mom told me to be a doctor."

Tamanna, 5
Kindergartner
Calcutta, India

Never underestimate the power of a smile.
Smiles cross all boundaries.

As a dentist, Pramila Murthy encounters a whole lot of people who, because of neglecting their teeth, are unable to smile. She takes great pride in putting smiles back on her patients' faces.

"Everyone owes it to themselves to look and feel their best every day. It sounds simple enough, yet it is too often overlooked, which is why I carve out some time for myself every day. I do something daily to engage my mind, strengthen my body and nurture my soul. Most importantly, I make it a point to bring laughter into my life and to bring a smile to those around me each and every day. This is when I feel my best.

I happen to be in a field where people are often terrified of visiting me, and so it is important to keep a smile on my face throughout the day. As a dentist, I have learned how powerful a smile can be. I once treated a patient who told me he had not smiled in years because he had been too ashamed by the appearance of his teeth. I was saddened at the thought of someone being unable to express happiness through a smile or laughter. He graciously thanked me for giving him back his smile. What a gift to be able to give the power and potential of a smile back to someone. This is why I educate my patients to devote a few minutes every day to brushing properly and flossing regularly to keep their teeth healthy and strong. Realize the power of your smile. Smile big and smile often. That smile will go a long way, and it can carry you far. In my life, I have learned how a smile can touch a person's soul and that it can change someone's life. Making others happy brings happiness to my own life, and that makes me smile even more."

Pramila Murthy, 34
Dentist
Arlington, Virginia, United States

91

Aim to live a borderless life.
Learn to appreciate all genres of art and culture.

Amar Sachdev considers himself to be an appreciator of music. Through Deejaying, Amar is constantly experiencing and sharing new genres of music and culture.

"I learned a lot from my father through his experience as a classical Indian musician. He earned great respect for the purity of his music. He declined opportunities to commercialize, because he wanted to focus on the integrity of his own music. He played for himself and to share with people, not for profit or fame. When I was younger, I experimented with music, but never took it to a level of practicing daily. In the past few years, I began producing concerts for my dad and branched out into the global-music scene. When asked if I will follow in my father's footsteps as a musician, I respond, saying that I am an appreciator of music. It's important to have people who simply appreciate music. As a disc jockey, I play other people's recorded music, and I'm in touch with all genres. When I play, there are times that I'm so into the music and the energy of the crowd that I lose myself in the moment.

My dream is to experience as many cultures as I can in my lifetime. I want to immerse myself in as many cultures as possible. I bring my love for culture into the music I play, the events I plan and even the food I cook. People can experience the world through music and performance without ever knowing it. They can hear a song without knowing its origins, and years later, they may hear something similar in context and make a connection."

Amar Sachdev, 35
DJ & Global Gypsy
San Rafael, California, United States
(Originally from Jodhpur, India)

Vinita Voogd ventured into the United States after marriage. As the wife of a Holland native, the mother of two bicultural children and a woman of innumerable experiences who has traveled the world, Vinita expresses her multiculturalism through block art.

"As an artist, my hope is that people will understand the beautiful and complicated medium of print making. I started print making in 1982 and hope that I continue to grow and experiment within the medium. My images are influenced by my environment and by man's hand in changing this environment. I use everyday, mundane items to create my art and strive to change viewers' perceptions about our world. In the age of the extremes of wealth and poverty, peace and discord, technology and ecology, I try to create a landscape of harmony by blending cultural decorative motifs, color, texture and pattern. You can see the influence of my culturally collaged life in my works through color, pattern and subject matter. I cannot help but be represented by my art. It comes from within, it is me, it is personal!"

Vinita Voogd, 54
Block Artist
*Los Angeles, California United State*s
(Originally from New Dehli, India)

92 If you lose a loved one,
remember how they lived, not how they died.

Reflect on what you gained from having the person in your life for a period of time.

On October 27, 2005, Jorge Gonzalez received a phone call with news that his fourteen-year-old sister Nayanci had been shot and killed by a young man. When Jorge arrived at the scene, he realized that the phone call was real. Jorge will likely never come to terms with the loss of his baby sister, but he has made a conscious effort to celebrate the way that Nayanci's presence made the world a better place.

"When Nayanci died, part of my soul died along with her. Living without Nayanci sometimes feels like being a fish in a shallow pond. It takes all the strength I have to move, to go on. But I know I have to, because that's what Nayanci would want. Now, when I walk into her room, I see her things just as she left them. Part of me still hopes she'll walk into her room behind me. I still can picture Nayanci dancing and singing to her favorite music, turning up the music on her boom box to drive me crazy.

She had a smile that could make my worst day sunny and clear. Nayanci never let a day go by without telling my parents how much she loved them, and now I do the same. She greeted everyone and now I try to do that. She found the goodness of people and gave people the benefit of the doubt, and I hope someday to be able to do the same. Nayanci's life inspired me to do what I can to make the world a better place. I celebrate Nayanci's life by keeping the memories that we shared alive, by helping people see the world in a different way. I am developing a program for high-school girls and boys in Nayanci's honor. I want to teach young women to feel empowered to speak out and to teach young boys to respect girls and women. I hope that our world will no longer be blinded by hate and indifference, and that we can all learn to forgive each other."

Jorge Gonzales, 22
Student
Oakland, California, United States

This is an excerpt of the poem Nayanci read to her English class the week before she died. Jorge reads this poem in his sister's honor when he talks with men and women about respectful relationships.

Nayanci G

When tomorrow starts without me and I'm not there to see;
If the sun should rise and find your eyes all filled with tears for me...
I wish so much you wouldn't cry the way you did today, while thinking of so many things we didn't get to say.
I know how much you loved me, as much as I love you. And each time that you think of me, I know you'll miss me too.
But when tomorrow starts without me please try to understand that an angel came and called me name and took me by the hand, and said my place was ready in heaven far above, and that I'd have to leave behind all those I truly loved.
If I could relive yesterday just even for a while, I'd say goodbye and kiss you and maybe see you smile. So when tomorrow starts without me, don't think we're far apart, for everytime you think of me, I'm right here in your heart.

Author Unknown

163

Never let fear paralyze you.

With just one life to live, you simply don't have time to let your fears stop you or interfere with your dreams and visions.

I met Kim Vu on the day I handed in the first draft of my manuscript to my publisher. She shared her life story as she gave me a manicure and a pedicure and helped me remember why I started this project in the first place. After the Vietnam War, Kim remembers her family and her neighbors living in constant fear. Kim's family had owned a bike shop. Kim's mother threw everything that the family owned in the river in the middle of the night. Under the new political system, it was believed that you couldn't own more than your neighbor without facing dire consequences. Kim knew that if she stayed, she would continue to feel like a prisoner; and if she left, she risked being imprisoned, dying or getting killed. Kim decided she had nothing to lose. It took Kim three tries before she was successfully able to leave. She was imprisoned on two occasions and shot at once, but once she left, she never looked back.

"I arrived in the United States on September 13, 1989 by myself, without a penny in my pocket. I couldn't speak English or say anything other than 'yes' or 'no.' I needed to start earning money right away, so I could support myself and my family.

I didn't have the time or means to go to college, but I learned from my friend that I could study for three-and-a-half months to get my license to do nails, and that is what I did. I went to school in the day and worked as a waitress in the Tenderloin district of San Francisco in the evening. I started working in a nail salon the day after I graduated, and after a few years, I took $8,500 (every penny I saved since arriving) and bought a nail salon. I wasn't scared, because I already knew that if I lost the money, I would work hard and get it back. After I got pregnant with my son, I sold my business to my employee. In 1994, I came to Marin and began renting a station for doing nails at a hair salon. In 2000, I bought my own shop in San Rafael, and most of my clients came with me.

I feel proud to be making it here on my own and to be able to help support my family in Vietnam. I have had to make sacrifices. I lost my father without having a chance to say goodbye, and I'm losing my mom, who is very ill. I keep asking my mom to wait for me until next summer when I can afford to go back and visit her one last time. I'm married to my business. Ninety

percent of my customers treat me like a family member. I feel like I do something to make people happy, and that makes me happy. Some of my customers come in each time they have a fight with their significant other or a co-worker. While I give them manicures and pedicures, I listen and talk with them about my own life. One of my customers, who is going through a divorce, is scared about starting over and sacrificing the high-end lifestyle she knew with her husband. I tell her that if I can make it, she can make it. I want people to know what people go through to get to the United States. If people are scared, I want them to read my story and know that if I can make it, others can too. If you can't get your dream job, start with any job, even if you have to take a smaller salary and work your way up. I want my son to know that life's not easy. If you have a goal and work hard enough, while setting your fears aside, you'll get it. When you finally accomplish your goal, you'll be proud and appreciate everything you have."

Kim Vu, 41
Esthetician, Manicurist & Pedicurist
San Rafael, California, United States
(Originally from Cantho, Vietnam)

165

Learn to put yourself first.

The better you treat yourself, the better you'll treat the world.

Raina Racki has traveled the world, while doing Baha'i service in each of her respective destinations and sharing her talents as a performing artist with the world. At the age of thirty-two, Raina has decided to take a step in a new direction—she is becoming a tropical horticulturist. Through her life journey, Raina has learned that the most important thing she can do is be honest with herself, have a forgiving spirit and be intentional about taking care of herself.

"I got married when I was twenty-three, and I was divorced by the time I was twenty-five years old. I remember noticing that I wasn't comfortable with parts of our relationship before we got married, and I wasn't following my intuition. Our relationship started falling apart, and my husband started pulling away. I fought it, thinking I could make our relationship work—and then I realized it was really a matter of self-preservation. I thought I'd done something wrong, betrayed myself, and that is the ultimate personal torture. For a long time, I felt regretful and negative, and then I realized that I'm not perfect and that nobody is. If I don't forgive myself and my ex-husband, it holds me back and stops me from seeing the wonderful possibilities that are in front of me. I needed to shut the door and move on. I'm in

a relationship now with a man who wants to marry me and I have to go very slow and be sure, so that I can trust myself. I have to heal from past hurts at the same time as I grow and move forward.

I am rejoicing in the learning process and learning to honor myself, take care of myself and 'put me first.' By honoring myself, I can honor others as well and be a more productive person. Sometimes I think women are conditioned to be like octopuses, throwing our tentacles all over the place to take care of everyone else first, and because of that, we're not grounded. If we can bring our energy into the middle, center ourselves and ask ourselves what we need, how we can take care of ourselves physically, emotionally and spiritually, then we'll be more effective individuals, parents, partners, sisters and daughters. I'm intentional about getting enough sleep, and it cures everything (or at least makes it all more manageable). I make time every morning and evening for prayer and reflection. One of the things that my faith encourages is to call ourselves to account each day, taking time to reflect on what went well, what we can improve on. I call myself to account every evening and it is wonderful for keeping me on track. I eat healthy food and eat regularly and try to

integrate physical exercise—yoga, dance, gardening and farm work—into my life every day. If everyone in the world forgave themselves for what has gone wrong and got in the practice of putting themselves first, I am convinced the level of joy in the world would max out. We'd all be more creative, productive and open with others, and our hearts would be lighter."

Raina Racki, 32
Farmer, Tropical Horticulture Student &
Performing Artist
Hilo, Hawaii, United States

95 Live graciously.

No matter how much money you make or what geographic location you are in, strive to live with class.

John Patrick Gill created a winery in a working-class community in the heart of Wisconsin. His vision was to introduce gracious living to people of all walks of life.

"I worked as a mechanical engineer for many years. Being an engineer is like being a male. Once a male, always a male. As a result, I was very left-brained. I set out to learn how to get in touch with the right side of my brain so I could enjoy the most simple things in life. This made me especially passionate about learning the art of gracious living. When I turned sixty-five, I got laid off. That was my opportunity to reassess life. I had always had a passion for wine and enjoyed making it as a hobby. I decided to turn my passion into a business. My wife and I bought a farm surrounded by beautiful, rolling hills and created a winery right in the heart of Wisconsin. I wanted to introduce fine wine to local people at a reasonable price and inspire them to live graciously.

My saying is "in vino veritas." In wine, truth. There is nothing better than sitting in the shade on a ninety-eight degree day, overlooking the quiet, beautiful, rolling hills and sharing a bottle of wine with a friend. You'll get politically incorrect and pour your heart out. It's a wonderful shared experience. Gracious living can be found at any socioeconomic level. People in Hollywood have it all wrong. I have a friend in Malibu who has liposuction once a month to maintain a certain aesthetic. That is not gracious living. Gracious living is quietude, good conversation, fine wine and nature. As for winemaking, I put materials together, and then a higher power takes over to convert them into wine. In vino veritas. In wine, truth."

John Patrick Gill, 70
Enalogist (Wine Scientist)
Blair, Wisconsin, United States

Strive to celebrate life every day.

Drop your inhibitions and follow the beat of your soul.

Pope Flyne started playing with the drums as a child and never stopped. Pope was invited to bring his talents to the United States in 1986, when the city of Oakland, California made Pope's hometown of Takoradi, Ghana its sister city. Through the simple instrument of the drum, Pope remembers to celebrate life every day.

"I grew up in a village, with no electricity and no connection to the outside world other than radio. The only toys you could have as a kid, were those that you could make by yourself, out of ordinary items. The first toy someone made for me was a drum. Once I started playing, I never stopped. I express myself better on the drums than any other way. In my village, the drum is an essential. It is still used as a means for sending messages, calling a meeting, holding a gathering or even finding a child that is lost in the vast African forest. Everyone remembers to gather when they hear the drums. My tribe has a festival of harvest called Kundum that happens every September. The festival goes on for days and everyone eats for free. On the sixth day, people meet the elders and talk with them about their problems. On the seventh day during the night, everyone picks up a rock and walks to the beach to participate in a ritual of forgiveness. By releasing the rock, people agree to let the past be gone and start fresh.

Now, when I teach my students to dance to the beat of African drums, I want them to understand that the drum has a language of its own. It inspires people to dance, to get exercise and gives people a lens for understanding the culture of Africa. Every human being has the ability to dance. African dance teaches you about rhythm and power. Once you understand rhythm, there's no dance that you can't do."

Pope Flyne, 59
Master Drummer, Choreographer & Singer
Tracey, California, United States
(Originally from Takoradi, Ghana)

Follow your inner compass.

Your core values and instincts give you the guidance necessary to live the life that is most true to you.

After learning that his father had Lou Gehrig's disease and only months to live, Monoo Prasad, who at the time was living and working in London, didn't think twice about what to do. As the eldest son, he wanted to be there for his father. Monoo cut his project short, set aside the independence that came along with his bachelor status and moved home. The experience of being at his father's side throughout a terminal illness forever changed Monoo.

"The experience sped up my maturation process. My parents reached out to me, and I was there. I watched my dad deteriorate. First, he started slurring, then he lost strength in his voluntary muscles and, eventually, it became hard for him to talk. After his ability to walk went away, my dad decided he didn't want to continue living and stopped eating and drinking, and on October 26, 2003, he passed away. I learned from my father's courage that money, wealth and status don't matter. What matters is family, relationships and strength within yourself—to know yourself, to be yourself, to follow your inner compass."

Monoo Prasad, 30
Engineering Manager
Milpitas, California, United States
(Originally from Bihar, India)

Learn the art of compromise.

We all have different ideas about the way things ought to be done and are prone to misunderstandings. Remember that your way is not necessarily the better way, and nobody is perfect.

Masai Suzuki and Harris Erwanto come from completely different walks of life. Masai was studying comparative cultural studies at Sophia University in Tokyo, and Harris was a contract worker from Indonesia. The two met during a social event at Masai's college. They started dating, and soon after, they got married.

"Sometimes, it's hard for us. We come from different cultures with different lifestyles, different religions, different ways of thinking and different personalities. Since we both have different native languages, sometimes we misunderstand each other and get into arguments. It's getting easier, though. We are learning about each other's cultures and learning to compromise."

Harris Erwanto, 32
Contract Worker
Tokyo, Japan
(Originally from Jakarta, Indonesia)

By virtue of coping with more than one language, culture and life style, intercultural couples may be more familiar with the value of compromise than anyone else. Shibuya Ujiro is a mentor for intercultural couples in Japan.

He recognizes that life is challenging for international spouses in the homogenous country. However, he says once intercultural couples get past their struggles and learn to compromise, they are bound to have more interesting lives. The same advice is applicable to people of all backgrounds and all types of relationships.

"I've traveled the world and spent time in South America, Sri Lanka and the U.S. There are a lot of really interesting people in the world. There are more and more international people who, for one reason or another, find a Japanese spouse and stay in the country. I mentor intercultural couples to help them work through the difficulties they are facing. If you think about it, you can learn a lot about another culture and another way of life by being in an intercultural marriage. Aside from the difficulties and misunderstandings that sometimes arise, it could be very enjoyable."

Shibuya Ujiro, 42
Writer & Sociologist/
Intercultural Marriage Mentor
Saitama, Japan

Never sacrifice yourself, your goals or your dreams for the sake of others.

The most amazing people in life appear by chance when you are least expecting them and will not stand in your way.

Supriya was among the first women to join the Indian Air Force. While pursuing her passion, she met her life partner. Supriya knows that it's possible to be a wife and a mother without sacrificing her own self.

"My father used to take me to air shows when I was a child. I used to cover my ears and be afraid of the sound, but look up at the sky and be fascinated. By the time I was six years old, I knew I wanted to be a pilot in the Indian Air Force. It was a big no-no for girls to join the army, and a lot of people discouraged me. I would ask everyone why it wasn't okay and insist that I was capable of doing the job. I would say, 'Tell me I cannot do this when I fail, but give me a chance.'

When I was sixteen, I realized the easiest thing to do would have been to become a commercial pilot, but that was not financially feasible, and my parents were not keen on me trying to pursue this type of a career. My parents told me that I had to complete a basic education first and then they would think about it. They were hoping like hell that I would change my mind. But I got my BS in physics to appease my parents and never lost sight of my dream, and in 1993, I joined the National Defense Academy in Pune. Once I joined, there were many obstacles. I would complete the whole course, and then my instructor would tell me I wasn't performing up to my potential, and then I'd have to start from scratch. I made it through my course and became a transport pilot in 1995. I met my husband during training. We were both passionate about flying and each other. One day he told me had a crush on me, and then quickly corrected himself to say that he was in love with me and wanted to get married. We courted for two years before marrying. He was a fighter pilot and I was a transport pilot. Each night, we would exchange stories about our days. I would pour my heart out, and he would offer me the simplest of solutions. In 1999, both my husband and I were active in the conflict with Pakistan. It was during that year that I became the first female pilot to fly in Meh, the highest airfield in India. My husband supported me all the way through; we were far from a stereotypical marriage where the wife is a second-class citizen in the home. Instead, we divided up housework according to who came home first. We even talked about someday being 'buddy pilots.' On August 5, 2000, my husband had to deliver an aircraft to New Delhi. When he was taking off, a bird got caught in the engine. He was able to get the plane to the ground, but before he could be rescued, the plane caught on fire with him inside, and I lost him. Our son was only six months old at the time. I feel so lucky to have spent six beautiful years of my life with this man. For my son's sake and for mine, I knew I had to be strong, so I dusted my pants, wiped my tears and kept going."

Supriya Gurjar, 34,
Retired Member of the Indian Airforce
Pune, India

 **100** Know that you are capable of inspiring someone with your story, your experience or your dream.

Reflect on who and what inspired you to the be the person you are today and create your own lesson or philosophy of life to guide you.

Share your lessons with the world.
www.interculturalencounters.com

Special Acknowledgements

A special thanks to:

- my mom for daring to dream big with me and providing me with endless support.
- my dad for helping me to develop a unique perspective on life.
- my sister for being my soul mate.
- the students, staff and faculty at Saint Mary's College of California, who inspire me every day.
- Deepak Srivastava and Saima Haque for designing my book.
- Nirmala Nataraj for countless hours of editing and encouragement.
- the entire *Nirvana Woman* team for being amazing colleagues.
- the *Asian American Press* in St. Paul, Minnesota, the *University Chronicle* at St. Cloud State University and the Twin Cities Journalist Fund for helping me kick off my journalism career.
- Vicki Virk for helping me discover my passion for Bhangra.
- the individuals who provided me with support during various phases of this project: Albert Filice, Collin Krauthamer, Farah Ahmad, Gabriella, Gordon Goff, Ilia Rodriguez, Janine Poehlman, Jayashree Patil, Jayne Bender, Jaz Banga, Jen Strass, Jeremy Splinter, Lindsey Rosellini, Loveleen Dhillon, Mary Stanhope, Michael Vadnie, Mister Buttercup, Nilu Srivastava, Nigel Yorwerth, Sanjib Sah, Sarah Reichel, Semya Hakim, Timothy Kiwala, Catherine Gaviola, Matt Tuscon, James Persinger and many others.

About the Author

Sharon K. Sobotta is a freelance journalist, a dancer, the managing editor for *Nirvana Woman* magazine and the director of the Women's Resource Center at Saint Mary's College of California. She has contributed to a host of publications, including the *Asian American Press* in St. Paul, Minnesota, the *East Bay Express* in Berkeley, California, *Marie Claire* magazine in New York City and the *Oakland Tribune* in Oakland, California. Inspired by her humble beginnings as the product of a working-class family in Wisconsin, Sharon truly believes that every individual has a teachable story. She started traveling the world when she was seventeen-years-old, after receiving a scholarship from Kikkoman soy sauce, which enabled her to go to Japan. That trip inspired Sharon to learn Japanese and caused her to develop an incurable desire to travel the world. She has since visited countless countries and interviewed thousands of people from every walk of life.

Sharon is not your typical traveler. When she travels, she lives among the locals, volunteers, studies and, most importantly, interviews and writes about the local population of her respective destination. In *The Journey of Life: 100 Lessons from Around the World*, Sharon shares some of the most profound pieces of insight and stories she has collected on her global journey.

Sharon began her journalism career as a cultural and social-issues beat writer for the *University Chronicle* at St. Cloud State University in 1999 with the goal of making the world and its issues accessible to those who didn't have the chance to experience it first-hand. In Sharon's role as director of the Women's Resource Center at St. Mary's College of California, she strives to inspire students to look at gender issues through a global, non-xenophobic lens and as part of the larger social issues of privilege and oppression. When Sharon is not writing, traveling or directing the Women's Resource Center, she can most often be found on the dance floor performing Bhangra, Hula or Middle Eastern dance with her dance troupe.